A Lenten Journey

with Jesus Christ and

St. Paul of the Cross

An Invitation of Grace,

a Prayer of Hope,

and a Gift of Peace.

A LENTEN JOURNEY

with Jesus Christ and

ST. PAUL OF THE CROSS

Daily Gospel Readings

with

Selections from the Writings

of

St. Paul of the Cross

REFLECTIONS AND PRAYERS

BY

REV. VICTOR HOAGLAND, C.P.

WITH ADDITIONAL INTRODUCTORY MATERIAL BY

PETER J. MONGEAU

WELLESLEY, MA

www.ChristusPublishing.com

Christus Publishing, LLC
Wellesley, Massachusetts
www.ChristusPublishing.com

Father Victor Hoagland, C.P, preaches at parish missions and retreats for priests, religious, and laity throughout the United States and is the director of Passionist Press, which publishes material pertaining to the Passionists and their ministry. A member of the U.S. Passionists' eastern province, he studied at the Catholic University of America and the Gregorian University in Rome. Afterwards, he taught liturgy, sacramental theology, and spirituality to seminarians of his own community and at St. John's University, Queens, New York. He also served in the provincial administration of his province.

Peter J. Mongeau is the Founder and Publisher of Christus Publishing, LLC.

Publisher's Cataloging-in-Publication Data
Hoagland, Victor
   A Lenten Journey with Jesus Christ and Saint Paul of the Cross: daily Gospel readings with selections from the writings of St. Paul of the Cross: reflections and prayers / by Victor Hoagland ; with additional introductory material by Peter J. Mongeau.
   p. ; cm.

   Includes bibliographical references.
   ISBN: 978-0-9841707-5-3

   1. Lent--Prayers and devotions. 2. Paul, of the Cross, Saint. 3. Paul, of the Cross, Saint --Prayers and devotions. 4. Catholic Church--Prayers and devotions. 5. Passionists--Prayers and devotions. 6. Prayer books. I. Mongeau, Peter J. II. Title.

BX2170.L4 P63 2010
240/.34   2011920099

Printed and bound in the United State of America

10   9   8   7   6   5   4   3   2   1

Text design and layout by Peri Swan
This book was typeset in Garamond Premier Pro with Snell Roundhand as a display typeface

CONTENTS

Acknowledgments ✦ 1

Dedication ✦ 2

An Invitation from St. Paul of the Cross ✦ 3

St. Paul of the Cross: A Short Biography ✦ 5

The Writings and Spirituality of St. Paul of the Cross ✦ 13

The Passionists: A Brief History ✦ 16

On the Daily Gospel Readings ✦ 20

Ash Wednesday and the Days after Ash Wednesday ✦ 25

First Week of Lent ✦ 37

Second Week of Lent ✦ 61

Third Week of Lent ✦ 83

Fourth Week of Lent ✦ 105

Fifth Week of Lent ✦ 131

Holy Week ✦ 159

Paschal Triduum ✦ 197

Easter Sunday ✦ 215

Epilogue ✦ 219

APPENDIX A:
Calendar of Lent 2011–2020 & Lectionary Cycle ✦ 221

APPENDIX B:
Selections from the Writings of St. Paul of the Cross ✦ 226

Suggestions for Further Reading ✦ 228

Internet Resources ✦ 230

Cover Art ✦ 232

About the Author ✦ 233

ACKNOWLEDGMENTS

The Gospel passages are taken from the *Lectionary for Mass for Use in the Dioceses of the United States of America, second typical edition* © 2001, 1998, 1997, 1986, 1970 Confraternity of Christian Doctrine, Inc., Washington, DC. Used with permission. All rights reserved. No portion of this text may be reproduced by any means without permission in writing from the copyright owner.

The citations from the works of St. Paul of the Cross are taken from *Words from the Heart: A Selection from the Personal Letters of St. Paul of the Cross,* Dublin, 1976, and from *Letters of Saint Paul of the Cross,* 3 vols., translated by Roger Mercurio, C.P. and Frederick Sucher, C.P., edited by Laurence Finn, C.P. and Donald Webber, C.P., Hyde Part, NJ, 2000, with revised translations by the author herein. Reprinted with permission.

DEDICATION

To the Passionist men and women who have followed their Holy Founder into the dark places of the world with the Word of the Cross.

REV. VICTOR HOAGLAND, C.P.

AN INVITATION FROM ST. PAUL OF THE CROSS

Imagine you lived in the eighteenth century in the small city of Pitigliano in Central Italy in the Tuscan Maremma. What was Pitigliano like then? Well, the word "Maremma" means "swampland." Pitigliano was a city built on a hill above swampland. Like the rest of the Maremma then, its economy was in tatters from years of wars and fighting. Foreign armies made the Maremma a battleground to win territory in Italy—nothing valuable to worry about there, they thought. The rich fled to the safety of big cities like Siena and Florence; the governments in charge were not much help.

It's March 1732 and the roads, often impassible and bandit-ridden, are muddy from the spring rains. Poor migrants are arriving to cultivate the fields left untended due to the wars. What if they get sick? We hardly have enough food to feed ourselves, the people of Pitigliano think. What are we going to do with the beggars at our churches and knocking on our doors?

In the town square before the church they put up a platform. Two men in black garments carry a cross to it. One is Paul Danei; the other is his brother John Baptist. Paul holds up the cross before the people who come to hear him preach. It's a Lenten mission and he tells them the story of the One who hangs on the cross. His listeners see themselves and their small city in the story he tells, and their hearts begin to burn within them. The missionaries hear confessions and settle some family feuds; they stay for thirteen days or so then move on to another town and place.

I wish I could tell you conditions changed for the better in Pitigliano after the two brothers preached, but they didn't. Mosquitoes still brought disease from the swamplands, the economy didn't get much better, the roads didn't get paved and the poor still roamed the city.

But the preaching of the two brothers helped the people of Pitigliano look at themselves and their lives differently. God was with them. They also remembered the two preachers and wanted them to come back again.

If St. Paul of the Cross—Paul Danei, founder of the Passionists—were to accompany you through Lent I'm sure he would come to you as you are and the world you live in as it is. He was never afraid of darkness or dark places, so you may find him a helpful spiritual guide. He trusted in Jesus Christ and his cross, "the wisdom and power of God." I'm sure he may bring some of that wisdom to you.

ST. PAUL
OF THE CROSS:
A SHORT
BIOGRAPHY

ST. PAUL OF THE CROSS 1694–1774

"Tell me the landscape on which you live and I'll tell you who you are" (Ortega y Gasset).

In 1714 a young northern Italian, Paolo Danei, had a striking experience of God. It happened during an ordinary sermon in an ordinary church, preached by an unknown parish priest. A sense of God and a desire to serve him filled his heart. Over the years, the experience grew and centered on the Passion of Jesus Christ.

From the sermon he heard in church, the young man gained a life-long respect for preaching. In his early years he taught catechism in churches near his home; later he became a powerful preacher of God's word.

In 1715, responding to a call for help from the pope, Paul left his work helping his father to join a crusade against the Turks who were threatening the Venetian Republic, but he soon realized that God wasn't calling him to be a soldier. There was something else for him to do, and so he returned to help in the family business.

"MY FATHER WAS A POOR TOBACCONIST"

His father was a poor tobacconist who moved his family and small store from town to town near Genoa trying to make ends meet. Financial conditions in Italy were bad as economic power shifted from the Mediterranean to the Atlantic coast, bringing prosperity to the seaports of England, Holland, and France, but leaving Italy, once the richest country in Europe in Renaissance times, a poorer place.

Considered medicinal at the time, tobacco was an item that hardpressed governments put a high tax on. Paul's father fell into the clutches of zealous Italian tax-collectors more than once as he brought supplies for his store from the docks of Genoa. No doubt his son did too. Paul would always have a soft spot in his heart for people in trouble with the law.

The Danei were a devout Catholic family. Large families were not unusual then. They had sixteen children; Paul was the second child, born in the town of Ovada on January 3, 1694. Only six children survived into their adult years; the majority died as infants. So Paul Danei became acquainted early on with the mystery of death, and from his mother especially, he learned to see it through the lens of the Passion of Christ.

"POOR ITALY"

"Poor Italy," Paul called his native land, and in the eighteenth century it was poor in more ways than one. The majority of its people lived in rural areas hit hard by the country's weak economy. Many were illiterate.

Politically, the Italian peninsula was a patchwork of small city states and territories that made it easy prey for Europe's bigger states coveting its resources. The governments of Spain, France, and Austria continually found reasons to meddle in Italian affairs and periodically sent their armies across its borders to enforce their will. Outside control made it difficult for Italy to develop economically and politically.

The Catholic Church also shared in eighteenth-century Italy's poverty. The popes controlled large sections of the Italian peninsula—the ancient Papal States—but they were under the thumb of foreign powers. Foreign rulers already had their hands in appointing bishops and in the affairs of religious orders; through agents they manipulated papal conclaves to lessen the role of the papacy in European politics. If they couldn't get a pope that favored them, they settled for an old man in poor health, less likely to get in their way. Their aim, already realized in England by Henry VIII and his ministers in the sixteenth century, was to weaken the ancient church, dismantle its religious orders and institutions, and grab its wealth for themselves.

Historians recognize the limitations big governments placed on the papacy in the eighteenth century: the popes of the era were "good men," "spiritual leaders," but—with the exception of Benedict XIV—lacking the "breadth of understanding" to deal with the critical problems of their times (Henri Daniel-Rops). They were "humane," "not heroic," "mostly good-humored" church leaders caught in the whirlwind of changing times (Owen Chadwick). They held on to the past, but were not sure how to face the future.

Paul Danei saw the popes of his day, vulnerable as they were, as the vicars of Christ on earth. They were part of the spiritual landscape of his time.

THE ENLIGHTENMENT

Beside political and economic forces, a new movement, the Enlightenment affected eighteenth century Italy and the rest of Europe, as well as Europe's colonies in the New World. Scientists, philosophers, and historians saw human reason as the way to a better future and emphasized human rights and human and scientific development—values they've passed on to us today. The Enlightenment changed the spiritual landscape of the western world.

The movement's followers were religious, for the most part, though some, like the French philosopher Voltaire, attacked religion (especially the Catholic Church) as the chief enemy of human progress and denied God's existence.

Most figures of the Enlightenment, like the Americans, George Washington and Thomas Jefferson, believed in a "providential deism." God created the world, yet afterwards watched it from a distance. No need, the deists thought, for revealed religions or for prayer or spiritual searching into a higher world. This world's secrets discovered through science and reason are enough:

> Know then thyself,
> presume not God to scan;
> the proper study of mankind is man
> > (ALEXANDER POPE, ESSAY ON MAN).

Enlightenment thinkers, whose God was little involved in human affairs, would dismiss a spiritual awakening like Paul Danei's. Human growth took place through human effort, not from heavenly grace.

THE "ENLIGHTENMENT" AT CASTELLAZZO

Yet, Paul Danei saw himself guided from above, mostly by slow steps and small graces, with occasional strong spiritual experiences. God was close, he believed, but mostly in a dark closeness. The young man regularly prayed and read the scriptures and spiritual books to know God's will, but the road to take wasn't clear.

He faced unanswered questions all his life. Who would support his struggling family? Should be marry? An uncle, a priest, tried arranging a good marriage for him, but he declined the offer. Sometimes his faith seemed to disappear. But then, on a trip for supplies for the family's store, he would see a mountain shrine and hear a call to "climb the mountain of the Lord."

Six years after the sermon in church, another strong experience of God occurred. "In the summer of 1720, at the time of the grain harvest, after communion at the Capuchin church in Castellazzo on a street corner near my home—I was raised up in God in the deepest recollection with complete forgetfulness of all else and with great interior peace." He saw himself clothed in a black garment with a white cross on his breast on which was written the name of Jesus.

He told his family and then the bishop of his diocese that he wished to be clothed in the garment of a hermit a common step for those wishing to serve God in those days. Then he settled in a small room belonging to the church of St. Charles in Castellazzo and for forty days he fasted and prayed to know what further step to take.

His diocesan bishop, Bishop Francesco Gattinaro, asked Paul to keep a diary of those days, and Paul afterwards gave him a written account of moments of great consolation and great emptiness. It was what he would experience for the rest of his life. At the end of the forty days, like Jesus in the desert, he embraced a mission. He believed God was calling him to begin a new community in the Church.

The eighteenth century wasn't favorable for founding new religious communities, however. Governments considered some existing religious communities, like the Jesuits as dangerous political adversaries; others, as socially useless. And Henry VIII had already shown that lands appropriated from religious communities could bring in healthy sums.

Facing economic hard times, the Church wasn't looking for new religious communities either; there were more than enough, most church leaders thought.

So instead of supporting Paul's desire to found a new community, Bishop Gattinaro told him to take charge of the little chapel of S. Stephano in Castellazzo. Within months the young hermit had renewed the people of the area spiritually with his words and spiritual advice, and other young men began to associate with him as companions.

GOING TO ROME

By the summer of 1721, Paul wrote to the bishop "I feel inspired by God to go to Rome." In late September, he was at the door of Quirinal Palace, where the pope then resided, and asked to see the Holy Father.

A new pope had just been elected, Innocent XIII (1721–24), "a well-meaning but sickly old man" who would be bedridden for much of his papacy. The guards at the palace door told Paul to go away.

The young man, who thought he would be received with open arms, made his way dejectedly toward the basilica of St. Mary Major not far from the Quirinal Palace, and before the church's ancient icon of Mary, Help of the Roman People, asked for help to do God's will and placed his cause in her hands. Then, he started home.

A HOLY MOUNTAIN: MONTE ARGENTARIO

On the boat to Rome, Paul's eyes were drawn to a majestic mountain that dominated the coast not far from the city, Monte Argentario. Perhaps, he thought after the rejection at the papal palace, this might be the place where God would speak more clearly to him.

In the spring of 1722 Paul and his brother, John Baptist, climbed Monte Argentario and moved into the abandoned hermitage of the Annunciation on the mountain's high slope. Here, they prayed and studied the Scriptures and let earth, sky and sea tell the story of creation to them. On Sundays the two went down the mountain to the little fishing villages along the water for Mass and afterwards taught catechism to the children.

As before, people responded to their words and soon not only children, but adults came to hear the two men. Their fame spread until priests and bishops were asking them to come and preach God's word in other towns and places. Eventually, the two brothers were welcomed to Rome where they found patrons in the Church's highest offices. For a brief period they ministered in one of Rome's hospitals and were advised to become priests. They were ordained in St. Peter's Basilica on June 7, 1727 by Pope Benedict XIII.

A NEW COMMUNITY IN THE CHURCH:
THE PASSIONISTS

The two brothers soon found, however, that they were not meant for that place, especially when new hospital directives called them to inflict painful health procedures on patients along with spiritual assistance. So, they returned to their beloved mountain to resume a life of prayer and preaching. Now their attention turned to the down-trodden towns and cities of the Tuscan Maremma and Papal States in central Italy.

The Tuscan Maremma, two thousand square miles of unhealthy coastal marshes stretching from the Mediterranean Sea to the mountain plains of the Apennines was a desperately poor area, unsafe because of bandits, unhealthy because of malaria and disease. Armies representing the dynasties of Europe and the feudal powers of Italy were garrisoned there and often battled to enforce their claims to the Italian peninsula. Periodic fighting caused the region's farmlands to be neglected, travel was dangerous and people sought safety behind the walls of their isolated communities.

Besides suffering from the consequences of war and politics, the area suffered from spiritual neglect. For years Paul and his brother, joined gradually by other companions, brought a message of hope to the dispirited men and women living in one of Italy's poorest regions.

Bishops, cardinals and popes began noticing the spiritual renewal these men brought about and gave them support. As others joined him, Paul sought places where they could be formed and from which they could go forth to preach. But the Church was painfully slow in approving the new community and Paul was an impatient prophet who "saw all things in God, but had no experience of how slow history can be" (G. Cingolani).

On May 15, 1741, twenty years after his first visit to Rome, his community's rule of life was approved by Pope Benedict XIV who said, "This congregation should have been first, but it is the last founded." On June 11, 1741, shortly after the approbation, the first six Passionists professed their vows, placing an emblem with a white heart and cross on the black habit they wore. Paul Danei started signing letters and documents "Paul of the Cross."

The message Paul and his followers preached was always the same: a loving God is near in Jesus Christ, who died for you. Keep his Passion in mind. In the poorest of places, in the poorest of humanity, God is present and brings his love.

Papal approval was no guarantee that the community would survive or go unchallenged, however. Some older religious communities considered the Passionists rivals for the scant support provided in hard times. Recruits for the new community came and went, especially in the beginning, but gradually membership grew and new foundations were made.

By 1752 Paul wrote, "We are 110. We have eight houses. They are all full and we cannot accept all those who want to join us."

He died in Rome, on October 18, 1775, acknowledged for his holiness and as a founder of a respected community in the Church. He was canonized a saint June 29, 1867.

THE WRITINGS
AND SPIRITUALITY
OF ST. PAUL
OF THE CROSS

"Please never stop writing me letters-they always manage to make me feel like my higher self" (Elizabeth Bishop, poet).

Letter-writing became popular in the western world in the eighteenth century, and St. Paul of the Cross diligently embraced the new medium to reach out to others. He wrote about ten thousand letters in his lifetime, though only two thousand or so survive. Just a few of his sermons remain, though he was a popular preacher always in demand for parish missions and retreats. He wrote no books, yet day after day, even when chronic illness kept him from doing anything else, he answered the stack of letters waiting for him on his desk. Besides his spiritual diary, which he wrote as a young man and is considered a spiritual classic, his letters are the best source of his spirituality.

His circle of correspondents was wide: church leaders, members of his own community, cloistered nuns, married and single men and women. He wrote to arrange for missions and retreats, to make requests for his new congregation, but most of his letter-writing was dedicated to spiritual direction.

Of Paul's over two thousand remaining letters, nine hundred were written to laypeople, the majority to women. Most of his correspondents were from the largely unhealthy Tuscan Marches of Central Italy, from the towns and cities perched on high ground above large swaths of malarial swamplands below. In these poor, incommodious places— Viterbo, Orbatello, Vetralla, Cecanno, Terracina, and other sites—Paul set up his first religious communities and met those seeking his advice and prayers.

Quotations from his letters to these individuals are found in this book; as you read them try to keep his correspondents in mind. They were mostly ordinary people; Paul never believed God called only the elite to holiness. There were constant correspondents like Thomas Fossi, a married businessman whose religious enthusiasm and wild religious schemes needed a steady hand. After his wife died, he became a Passionist priest. There was Lucy Burlini, a quiet, illiterate woman blessed by God with an exceptional gift of prayer, and the impetuous Agnes Grazi, whose religious imagination kept probing into a world beyond this. Some were plagued with scruples and temptations; others were caught in a web of daily trials. All came to Paul to lead them to God.

"I'm a blind guide," Paul said, claiming no special wisdom, yet people sought a holy man's reward from him. He was tender and blunt with them, enormously patient, because from his own experience he knew God works slowly, tenderly, sometimes bluntly. He never pretended to be learned, but depended on great spiritual guides like St. Teresa of Avila, St. John of the Cross, St. Francis de Sales and John Tauler for their wisdom, seldom quoting them explicitly.

Eighteenth century letter writers liked to explore life around them and letters were often the newspapers of the day. But Paul's letters were words for the soul; he wasn't interested in providing news or psychological advice or social analysis or counseling. His focus was helping people to pray. If they prayed his work was done; God would do the rest.

Every once in awhile, Paul recommends some human remedy in his letters; he himself went to the hot baths near Viterbo to ease his chronic pains. He knew a bit about Italian home medicines. At times, he points out flaws slowing someone's progress, but his letters have little of the moralizing, or self-help advice, or maxims of philosophical wisdom so popular in spiritual writing today. He began with suffering: the mystery present in ordinary human experience.

Paul responds to people's darkness: the doubts, fears, yearnings, and questions they have. You approach God in darkness: "Darkness and suffering can be your friends"; "faith comes alive in the dark." He's not interested in probing the causes of darkness; rather he discourages "philosophizing" or asking too many questions about it. "You shouldn't be looking at what you're going through and philosophizing minutely about it and reflecting so much on yourself . . . By thinking too much about yourself, you lose sight of the Sovereign Good."

A "High Providence" is at work in human darkness, Paul says, and the mystery of the Passion of Jesus is the way to respond to it. The mystery of the Cross, meditation on the Passion of Jesus Christ, leads to a strengthening self-knowledge and a transforming humility. The Passion of Jesus is the door into the Presence of God.

"I wish everyone could understand the great grace that God, in his mercy, sends when he sends suffering, especially suffering devoid of consolation. Then, indeed, we're purified like gold in the furnace. Without knowing, we become radiant and set free to fly to our Good, to a blessed transformation. We carry the cross with Jesus and don't know it."

An austere message? It's remarkably like the message found in the Paschal mystery we celebrate in Lent and Easter: Take up your cross and follow me, Jesus says, and you will find life. Lose your life and you will find it.

THE PASSIONISTS:
A BRIEF
HISTORY

PAUL'S LEGACY: THE PASSIONISTS

Born in critical times, in a poor country and a weakened church, Paul of the Cross was among the saints of the eighteenth century, like St. Alphonsus Liguori, St. Lucy Filippini, and St. Leonard of Port Maurice whom God raised up to bless the Italian Church and eventually the Church throughout the world.

From small beginnings, his community—the Passionists— spread to other continents where they're found today. Beside men, different groups of women, some cloistered, some dedicated to active ministry, became part of the Passionist family. Increasingly, lay people are drawn to the Passionist charism.

After Paul's death in 1774, the community's growth was halted by the Napoleonic suppression of religious communities in 1810. It almost disappeared. Reestablished in 1814, the Passionists were limited to Italy until 1840 when they expanded over a sixty year period into thirteen countries in Europe and America.

Before his death in 1771, Paul of the Cross founded a contemplative community of women, the Passionist Nuns. Later, active communities of Passionist women, among them the Sisters of the Cross and Passion, founded in England, were inspired by his charism. Their growth paralleled the growth of the community of men.

As the twenty-first century begins, the Passionist community is growing in Asia, Africa, and South America, while experiencing a decline in religious vocations in the western world.

Like their founder, the Passionists still reach out to poorer places of the world and lands where the Gospel needs to be preached. Inheritors of his charism, they face certain tasks in their mission today.

SPEAKING TO A FORGETFUL WORLD

The Passionists were founded as the Enlightenment began to change the western world and its religious traditions. In the saint's lifetime, it made slight inroads in Italy, which remained strongly attached to the ancient faith. Wayside crosses and newly built "Stations of the Cross" dotted the land. Devotion to Christ's Passion was fervent.

Yet Paul of the Cross saw radical changes ahead: "The world is sliding into a forgetfulness of the most bitter sufferings lovingly endured by Jesus Christ our true good."

With a mystic's insight Paul saw a slide that would lead to the secular age we live in today. The philosopher Charles Taylor in his book *The Secular Age* describes the secular age well. As Deism, the religion of the Enlightenment, minimized our ties to a higher world, people began to look to science and reason for the meaning of life. Deism is "a half-way house on the road to contemporary atheism," Taylor says. It has brought about a "forgetfulness" of God's revelation in Jesus Christ. Closing the heavens and making this life everything, it leads to the "expressive individualism" that drives so many today.

The Passionists wonder how they can remind a forgetful world today of the presence of God revealed in Jesus Christ who died on the cross and rose again? As they search for an answer they hear another favorite expression of their Founder: "Love is ingenious."

REMOVING THE CAUSES OF
HUMAN SUFFERING

The poor of Paul of the Cross's day were largely controlled by others and powerless to change the structures that caused them suffering. "I saw the name of Jesus written on the foreheads of the poor," Paul once said, but he could do little to reshape the structures that oppressed them.

Today, the church and other world institutions are increasingly aware of human rights and the need to relieve human suffering, especially of the poor. It is not enough to look for acceptance in the wisdom of the cross, but "strength to discern and remove the causes of human suffering." As they seek for justice, peace, and the integrity of creation, followers of Paul of the Cross are finding new challenges in his charism.

"We are aware that the passion of Christ continues in this world until he comes in glory; therefore, we share in the joys and sorrows of our contemporaries as we journey through life towards our Father. We wish to share in the distress of all, especially the poor and neglected; we seek to offer them comfort and to relieve the burden of their sorrow.

"The power of the cross, which is the wisdom of God, gives us strength to discern and remove the causes of human suffering" (Passionist Constitutions).

The natural world, too, lives today under the shadow of the cross because of human neglect. Paul Danei once chose to live on Monte Argentario, a mountain close to the sea where the hills, the sky and water reminded him of Infinite Goodness that created all things. Yet, he also saw great swaths of good land around him in the Tuscan Maremma destroyed by wars and human neglect.

Passionists today find in the cross and its redeeming power a call to respect the integrity of creation and care for its future.

PASSIONIST SAINTS

Since its recognition by the Church in the eighteenth century, the Passionist community has produced a remarkable number of saints and blessed. Besides its founder, St. Paul of the Cross whose cause for canonization was introduced shortly after his death, the community counts among its martyrs and holy men and women: Vincent Strambi, Gabriel Possenti, Gemma Galgani, Dominic Barberi, Isidore de Loor, Charles Houben, Lorenzo Salvi, Eugene Bossilkov, Innocent Canoura, and twenty-seven other Spanish martyrs.

They are witnesses to the holiness of the Passionist charism.

ON THE DAILY GOSPEL READINGS

This book presents daily readings and prayers for every day of Lent: Weekdays and Sundays. The daily readings begin with a Gospel Reading, followed by a reflection that contains a selection from St. Paul of the Cross's writings and a prayer.

The Gospel Readings are from the Roman Catholic *Lectionary for Mass for Use in the Dioceses of the United States of America*. The *Lectionary for Mass* contains the readings for Mass selected from the Bible.

If you were to attend daily Mass during Lent in the United States, you would hear the same Daily Gospel Readings included in this book. For example, the Ash Wednesday Gospel Reading, Matthew 6:1–6 and 16–18, is the same Gospel Reading you would hear when you attend Mass to receive your ashes. In fact, on each day at all the Masses of the Latin-rite Roman Catholic Church throughout the world, the same readings are heard in Mass, read in the vernacular language or Latin.

There are two main components of the Lectionary: Sunday and

Weekday readings. Sunday readings are arranged on a three-year cycle: Year A, Year B, and Year C. The Gospel Readings for Year A are generally from the Gospel of St. Matthew, Year B are generally from the Gospel of St. Mark, and Year C are generally from the Gospel of St. Luke. St. John's Gospel is read on Sundays in Year A, B, and C during specific liturgical calendar periods.

The Weekday readings are on a two-year cycle: Year I and Year II. Year I are odd-numbered years and Year II are even- numbered years. The Weekday readings during Lent are the same for Year I and Year II although each day's reading is different. In this book, the Weekday Gospel Readings are also the Weekday Gospel Readings in the Lectionary.

For Sundays in this book, you have three different selections of readings and prayers. Each selection begins with a different Gospel Reading, the Gospel Reading from Year A, B, or C of the Lectionary.

Appendix A, the Calendar for Lent 2011–2020 & Lectionary Cycle, lists the specific dates for the next ten years for Ash Wednesday, the Sundays of Lent, and includes the Sunday Lectionary Cycle for the year. Please refer to the table to determine the current year's Sunday Lectionary Cycle: Year A, B, or C and select the appropriate Sunday reading for the present year.

The Gospels and other readings in our Lenten Masses offer a grace to those who reflect on them day by day. It may help to look at the overall plan behind these readings, following the reforms of Vatican II.

THE SUNDAY GOSPELS

The Sunday Gospels of Lent are the most important guides to this season. The Gospel readings from Cycle A (also noted here as RCIA—Rite of Christian Initiation for Adults) are especially important for those preparing for baptism and those wishing to recall their own baptismal vocation.

First Sunday of Lent: The Temptation of Jesus, recalled by Mathew, Mark, and Luke, follows the account of Jesus' own baptism and is a vivid reminder that our baptismal life as Christians is similar to Christ's life: we are subject to trial and temptation.

Second Sunday of Lent: The Transfiguration of Jesus on the mountain is subject of all the Gospels and for the 2nd Sunday of Lent offers us the promise of light and glory even as we accompany him bearing our cross.

Third Sunday of Lent: In the story of the Samaritan Woman ("A" Cycle and RCIA) the gradual enlightenment of the woman by Jesus is a pattern of baptismal grace that steadily purifies and enlightens us. The "C" Cycle readings ask us to listen and respond to God's voice.

Fourth Sunday of Lent: The Man Born Blind ("A" Cycle and RCIA) shows the power of God offered to cure a helpless blind man. God's power is no less evident in the sacrament of baptism. The story of the prodigal ("C" Cycle) shows us how to find our way back from having gone terribly wrong.

Fifth Sunday of Lent: The Raising of Lazarus ("A" Cycle and RCIA) is a powerful reminder that Christ is the "resurrection and the life" and those who believe in him will have eternal life. The story of the woman charged with adultery ("C" Cycle) invites us to answer Jesus' invitation to walk in the light.

THE WEEKDAY GOSPELS

The Gospel of Matthew is the most frequently read of the four Gospels in the first three weeks of Lent, beginning with Ash Wednesday. Matthew's Gospel, an important catechetical tool in the early Church, still fulfills an important role today for preparing catechumens for baptism and renewing belief in those already baptized. In this Gospel, the confession of Peter at Caesarea, Philippi is the highpoint of the Gospel. "You are the Christ, the Son of the Living God," Peter says to Jesus, "You have the words of everlasting life." The purpose of Lent is to renew that confession in our hearts.

In Matthew's Gospel, Jesus begins his journey to Jerusalem from the Mount of the Beatitudes to the Mount of Calvary by urging his disciples to be faithful to prayer (Tuesday and Thursday, 1st week of Lent) and to love their neighbor, even their enemies and "the least" whom they might tend to overlook (Monday, Friday, Saturday, 1st week of Lent).

The love the Gospel proposes is not just an acceptable or normal love; it's a Godlike love. Jesus does not water down his challenge; his words raise our sights and set the bar for love higher than we like. Lent calls us to our best.

At the same time, this is the Gospel of Matthew the tax collector, as the reading for the Saturday after Ash Wednesday reminds us. Jesus called people like Matthew and his friends—not very good keepers of the law—to be his disciples. If we consider ourselves outsiders and sinners, welcome to the Lenten season. God's great mercy is at work.

The readings from St. Paul of the Cross accompanying these Lenten readings are often teachings about prayer, a frequent theme in the readings from Matthew and a major focus for our saint. "You fall away so easily by abandoning prayer. Never give it up." On the other hand, prayer is the way we approach God.

John's Gospel provides most of the Lenten weekday Gospels beginning with the 4th week of Lent. The Gospel was Paul of the Cross's favorite and he drew much of his spirituality from it. In John's theme of light shining in darkness he found a description of our spiritual journey. Our darkness is temptation and sin: yet the Word made flesh leads us to the Father to find rest in the light of his Presence, a rest we can enjoy even now through prayer.

The great stories from John's Gospel told in the final weeks of Lent reveal God's saving power in human weakness. The man born blind, the helpless paralytic, Nicodemus in the dark, Lazarus in the tomb represent humanity saved by the life-giving Word. The Gospel invites us to join this weak company to receive life through the power of God and share in his glory.

These stories remind us of our "nothingness," a favorite expression of St. Paul of the Cross. Only through humility and mystical death can we receive God's saving power. John's final story of the Passion and Resurrection of Jesus, which we read on Holy Thursday, Good Friday, and Easter Sunday: it is the final sign of this glorious mystery.

FR. VICTOR HOAGLAND, C.P.

PETER J. MONGEAU

"The world is sliding into a profound forgetfulness of the most bitter sufferings endured out of love by Jesus Christ, our true Good, while the memory of his most holy Passion is practically extinct among the faithful" (*Account sent to friends of the community, 1747*).

ST. PAUL OF THE CROSS

A S H
W E D N E S D A Y

*and the Days
after Ash Wednesday*

GOSPEL

JESUS SAID TO HIS DISCIPLES:

"Take care not to perform righteous deeds in order that people may see them; otherwise, you will have no recompense from your heavenly Father. When you give alms, do not blow a trumpet before you, as the hypocrites do in the synagogues and in the streets to win the praise of others. Amen, I say to you, they have received their reward. But when you give alms, do not let your left hand know what your right is doing, so that your almsgiving may be secret. And your Father who sees in secret will repay you.

"When you pray, do not be like the hypocrites, who love to stand and pray in the synagogues and on street corners so that others may see them. Amen, I say to you, they have received their reward. But when you pray, go to your inner room, close the door, and pray to your Father in secret. And your Father who sees in secret will repay you.

"When you fast, do not look gloomy like the hypocrites. They neglect their appearance, so that they may appear to others to be fasting. Amen, I say to you, they have received their reward. But when you fast, anoint your head and wash your face, so that you may not appear to be fasting, except to your Father who is hidden. And your Father who sees what is hidden will repay you."

MATTHEW 6: 1-6, 16-18

REFLECTION

On Ash Wednesday, ashes are placed on our foreheads in the form of a cross and simple words are said: "Remember you are dust and to dust you shall return." A reminder we will die. Yet, the brief symbolic act says so much more. A daily mystical death is also taking place within us. Our physical life will end, the ashes tell us; the day and hour are unknown. But ashes in the form of a cross tell us Jesus Christ changes death. "Dying, you destroyed our death. Rising, you restored our life." Jesus Christ has made his risen life ours. Though his gift is hidden, we will experience it when we enter his glory.

Meanwhile, the mystery of his death and Resurrection is at work in us now. Share this mystery mystically, St. Paul of the Cross says in a letter quoted below. Written during the celebration of the mystery of the birth of Jesus, the saint sees the cross as a sign of birth as well as a sign of death.

Daily, deliberately, attentively turn to God working within you, he says. A new life is being born in you, though you may not see it. Desire it; accept it in whatever God sends, without worry. God is working within through the mystery of the Lord's cross.

ST. PAUL OF THE CROSS

"Life for friends of God means dying each day: 'We die daily; for you are dead and your life is hidden with Christ in God.' This is the mystical death I want you to undergo. I'm confident that you will be reborn to a new life in the sacred mysteries of Jesus Christ, as you die mystically in Christ more and more each day, in the depths of the Divinity. Let your life be hidden with Christ in God . . .

"Think about mystical death. Dying mystically means thinking only of living a divine life, desiring only God, accepting all that God sends and not worrying about it. It means ignoring everything else so that God can work in your soul, in the sanctuary of your soul, where no creature, angelic or human, can go. There you experience God working and being born as you mystically die" (Letter 1766, December 29, 1768).

PRAYER

O Jesus, you place on my forehead
the sign of your saving Cross:
"Turn from sin and be faithful
to the Gospel."
How can I turn from sin
unless I turn to you?
You speak, you raise your hand,
you touch my mind and call my name,
"Turn to the Lord your God again."
These days of your favor
leave a blessing as you pass
on me and all your people.
Turn to us, Lord,
and we shall turn to you.
Amen.

GOSPEL

JESUS SAID TO HIS DISCIPLES:

"The Son of Man must suffer greatly and be rejected by the elders, the chief priests, and the scribes, and be killed and on the third day be raised."

Then he said to all, "If anyone wishes to come after me, he must deny himself and take up his cross daily and follow me. For whoever wishes to save his life will lose it, but whoever loses his life for my sake will save it. What profit is there for one to gain the whole world yet lose or forfeit himself?"

LUKE 9: 22-25

REFLECTION

Jesus offers a blunt challenge in this reading from Luke's Gospel; notice that he challenges all, not just his disciples. "If anyone wishes to come after me, he must deny himself and take up his cross daily and follow me."

No one escapes the cross that's there each day. We may not call it a cross; we may hardly notice it because it's so much part of life as we live it, but if we look closely we will find it. It may not look at all like the stark cross Jesus receives from the hands of the chief priests, the elders and the scribes in Jerusalem, but it's there all the same.

A traditional Christian practice is to make the Sign of the Cross as we begin the day. We do it to remind ourselves of the daily cross we bear and to remember that God gives us strength to bear whatever life holds that day. This Lent may be a good time to renew this basic Christian practice.

St. Paul of the Cross wrote the following letter to Teresa, who seemed worried about what's happening in her daily life, and urges her to let God's Will decide for her what to do. He wanted people to find their cross and embrace it:

ST. PAUL OF THE CROSS

"Teresa, listen to me and do what I'm telling you to do in the Name of the Lord. Do all you can to be resigned to the Will of God in all the sufferings that God permits, in your tiredness and in all the work you have to do. Keep your heart at peace and be recollected; don't get upset. If you can go to church, go; if you can't, stay quietly and contentedly at home; just do the Will of God in the work you have at hand" (Letter 1135, June 8, 1758).

PRAYER

Bless me, Lord,
and help me take up the cross
that's mine today.
Let me find you in the unexpected,
the unwelcomed, the unsettling things that happen,
the things that come for no reason at all,
except they come from your holy Will.
Amen.

GOSPEL

The disciples of John approached Jesus and said, "Why do we and the Pharisees fast much, but your disciples do not fast?" Jesus answered them, "Can the wedding guests mourn as long as the bridegroom is with them? The days will come when the bridegroom is taken away from them, and then they will fast."

MATTHEW 9: 14-15

REFLECTION

When you look at the length of human history, the years Jesus Christ lived on earth are brief. Yet, the Word made flesh came "in the fullness of time." His life, death, and Resurrection changed how we look at life and time itself.

During Lent we turn to him, "who is, who was and is to come." and ask him to lead us to eternal life.

His life and presence is a revelation we celebrate. His first disciples were his companions; they saw him, listened to his words and shared his presence. As friends of the bridegroom their experience of him was unique.

We don't know him as they did, but we know him by faith and through signs of his presence. The scriptures and the sacraments bring him to us. Love of others, especially of the least, reveal him. Lent is a time for celebrating the presence among us of Jesus Christ, truly divine and truly human.

"What a Christian should be doing at all times should be done now with greater care and devotion," Pope Leo the Great told believers beginning Lent in the sixth century. During Lent we turn to Jesus Christ, our way, our truth and our life.

In his spiritual diary, St. Paul of the Cross recognized the importance of the humanity of Christ. Meditation on his life, death, and Resurrection leads us to know him as divine. He brings us into contact with the Divinity.

ST. PAUL OF THE CROSS

"I also had knowledge of the soul united in a bond of love to the Sacred Humanity and, at the same time, dissolved and raised to a deep, conscious, and felt knowledge of the Divinity. For since Jesus is both God and Man, the soul cannot be united in love to the Sacred Humanity without being at the same time dissolved and brought to a deep, conscious, felt knowledge of the Divinity" (Spiritual Diary), January 1, 1721.

PRAYER

Thank you, Father, for the gift of your Son, Jesus Christ,
the Word who made the universe,
the Savior you sent to redeem us.
Let me follow him in his appearance among us,
from his birth in a stable
to his hidden life at Nazareth,
to his ministry in Galilee,
and finally to his death and Resurrection in Jerusalem.
Help me know him in his humanity
so that I may know him in his divinity.
Amen.

GOSPEL

Jesus saw a tax collector named Levi sitting at the customs post. He said to him, "Follow me." And leaving everything behind, he got up and followed him. Then Levi gave a great banquet for him in his house, and a large crowd of tax collectors and others were at table with them. The Pharisees and their scribes complained to his disciples, saying, "Why do you eat and drink with tax collectors and sinners?" Jesus said to them in reply, "Those who are healthy do not need a physician, but the sick do. I have not come to call the righteous to repentance but sinners."

LUKE 5: 27-32

REFLECTION

It's hard to imagine a more unlikely apostle than Levi, also called Matthew. Tax collectors, agents of a feared and hated government, were despised by ordinary Jews because they belonged to a profession considered greedy, unfair, and unclean. They were unwelcome in the synagogues and temple. No good Jew wanted to have anything to do with them.

Yet Jesus called Matthew and ate with him and his friends. Jewish leaders in Capernaum were outraged: "Why does he eat with tax collectors and sinners?" Jesus' answer is the answer of a merciful God. "The healthy don't need a physician, but the sick do."

There are no incurables among these sick either, no one whom God won't cure. Tax collectors are God's children and belong to God's family as anyone else does. The call of Matthew reminds us that in Lent God does not reach out to a favored few; he reaches out to the whole wounded world. So should we.

When St. Paul of the Cross preached missions in the towns of the Tuscan Maremma, he set up a platform in the village square to speak to all who came by. The crucifix he held high in his hands was a sign of God's mercy offered to all and denied to none. Bandits were common in Tuscan Maremma, and Paul brought many of these "unofficial Tax-collectors" back into society. Jesus wanted them to be saved.

ST. PAUL OF THE CROSS

"I rejoiced that our great God should wish to make use of so great a sinner . . . I tell my beloved Jesus that all creatures shall sing his mercies" (Spiritual Diary, November 27, 1720).

PRAYER

Lord,
who are the tax collectors I won't eat with
and the sick I won't heal?
Let me see them
and welcome them as you did;
they bring wealth and health,
richness and wholeness, to one as poor as me.
Amen.

FIRST WEEK
OF
LENT

GOSPEL

At that time Jesus was led by the Spirit into the desert to be tempted by the devil. He fasted for forty days and forty nights, and afterwards he was hungry. The tempter approached and said to him, "If you are the Son of God, command that these stones become loaves of bread." He said in reply, "It is written: / *One does not live on bread alone, / but on every word that comes forth from the mouth of God." /*

Then the devil took him to the holy city, and made him stand on the parapet of the temple, and said to him, "If you are the Son of God, throw yourself down. For it is written: / *He will command his angels concerning you / and with their hands they will support you, / lest you dash your foot against a stone." /* Jesus answered him, "Again it is written, *You shall not put the Lord, your God, to the test."* Then the devil took him up to a very high mountain, and showed him all the kingdoms of the world in their magnificence, and he said to him, "All these I shall give to you, if you will prostrate yourself and worship me." At this, Jesus said to him, "Get away, Satan! It is written: / *The Lord, your God, shall you worship / and him alone shall you serve." /*

Then the devil left him and, behold, angels came and ministered to him.

MATTHEW 4: 1-11

REFLECTION

Though scripture says Jesus was "like us in all things except sin," we tend to see him unlike us: a miracle worker, an assured teacher, master of the impossible. But look at him in the desert: weary, vulnerable, struggling in a dangerous land. Was most of his life like that?

Think how Jesus may have been tempted. To begin with, think of the demanding life he led, particularly in his ministry. People pressed upon him constantly. The blind man shouting from the roadside, the paralytic lowered from the roof, the woman pleading for her daughter—they're just some of the many who pressed their cares on him at every turn. Did he get tired doing good?

Certainly we do, even doing the best things. It's one of our greatest temptations.

Janet Erskine Stuart once wrote a poem about Jesus and the Samaritan woman at the well. He's tired out.

Lord, art thou weary? Is the work
the Father trusted to thy care,
his ruined temple to restore;
beyond thy mortal strength to bear?
Is thy omnipotence indeed
too sorely pressed in this our need?
Lord, art thou weary?

The Evil One's first suggestion to Jesus in the desert, that he turn stones into bread, is a temptation about power and control. We experience it too. Wouldn't it be wonderful to snap your finger and have everything done, without the weariness, the burden, the patient waiting most good things demand? Doing good day after day can be like pushing stones up a hill and wondering if we'll ever get there.

One good thing we can tire of is prayer. St. Paul of the Cross knew that temptation. Here's how he described it in his spiritual diary, which he wrote as a young man:

ST. PAUL OF THE CROSS

"I was dry, distracted and tempted. I had to force myself to stay at prayer. I was tempted to gluttony and seized with hunger. I felt the cold more than usual and wanted some relief, and on that account I wanted to flee from prayer. By the grace of God, my spirit held out, but the violence and assaults kept coming both from my flesh and the devil" (Spiritual Diary, December 10–13, 1720).

PRAYER

Lord,
when we feel our day becoming a desert,
and life beginning to be too much,
and we're tiring of doing good,
stay at our side and be our strength.
Amen.

GOSPEL

The Spirit drove Jesus out into the desert, and he remained in the desert for forty days, tempted by Satan. He was among wild beasts, and the angels ministered to him.

After John had been arrested, Jesus came to Galilee proclaiming the gospel of God: "This the time of fulfillment. The kingdom of God is at hand. Repent, and believe in the gospel."

MARK 1: 12-15

REFLECTION

Mark's narrative of the temptation of Jesus is brief, only two sentences.

Where does the story of the Temptation of Jesus come from, we wonder? It's hardly likely that the writers of the Gospel, or the Christian community itself, made up the story. More likely it came from Jesus himself who's describing his own experience—not just an experience of forty days, but in figurative language he's describing his experience of life.

He was human, "like us in all things except sin," and to be human means to be tempted. There was not a time when he didn't face opposition or challenge or lack of support in his life. It was not just the call to fulfill a prophet's role, like Elijah, that caused Jesus to be tempted; it was the human condition he shared with us.

To be human means that failure and sickness can crush our spirits; false values and promises can lead us astray. We're not always right or sure in the way we think and judge. We'd like to ignore temptation because it's a sign of human weakness, and we don't want to appear weak.

"Lead us not into temptation, but deliver us from evil," we say in the prayer Jesus prayed and taught us. God help us when we are tested, let us know the right thing to do, deliver us from evil.

In 1720, as a young man of twenty-six, Paul Danei made a retreat of forty days in the church of St. Charles in Castellazzo in northern Italy. His bishop and spiritual director, Bishop Gattinara, told him to keep a diary of his experiences, which he wrote in some detail.

He experienced temptations throughout the retreat, some he could name: temptations against faith, impatience, gluttony, impurity, but some he could only describe in general, such as "a particular kind of melancholy:"

ST. PAUL OF THE CROSS

"Hidden temptations which are hardly recognized as such. For this reason they afflict the soul very much. You don't know whether you are here or there, the more so because there is no sensible sign of prayer at this time. I realize that God enables me to understand that they purify the soul." (Spiritual Diary, November 23, 1720).

Paul's acceptance of temptation was an important part of his own spirituality and made him an excellent spiritual director of others. As the Lenten Gospels remind us, Jesus was tempted and so are we. Temptations are part of the mystery of the cross.

PRAYER

Lord,
help us to know you in these days of Lent,
your humanity, your life and death,
so like our own if we could see.
Help us to know ourselves,
frail creatures that we are,
tempted to evil,
and scarcely aware of what our temptations are.
Lead us on, by your grace, to your kingdom and eternal life.
Amen.

GOSPEL

Filled with the Holy Spirit, Jesus returned from the Jordan and was led by the Spirit into the desert for forty days, to be tempted by the devil. He ate nothing during those days, and when they were over he was hungry. The devil said to him, "If you are the Son of God, command this stone to become bread." Jesus answered him, "It is written, *One does not live on bread alone.*" Then he took him up and showed him all the kingdoms of the world in a single instant. The devil said to him, "I shall give to you all this power and glory; for it has been handed over to me, and I may give it to whomever I wish. All this will be yours, if you worship me." Jesus said to him in reply, "It is written: / *You shall worship the Lord, your God, / and him alone shall you serve.*" / Then he led them to Jerusalem, made him stand on the parapet of the temple, and said to him, "If you are the Son of God, throw yourself down from here, for it is written: / *He will command his angels concerning you, to guard you, /* and: / *With their hands they will support you, / lest you dash your foot against a stone.*" / Jesus said to him in reply, "It also says, *You shall not put the Lord, your God, to the test.*" When the devil had finished every temptation, he departed from him for a time.

LUKE 4: 1-13

REFLECTION

Luke's account of the temptation story of Jesus is roughly the same as Matthew's. The devil offers him all the kingdoms of the world if he will serve him.

The political and religious powers of the day certainly pressured Jesus to conform to their standards and be quiet. Just go along, they said, and we'll give you a place with us, even a place of honor. Jesus called them "children of the devil."

Even his own disciples advised him how to succeed. Listen to them: "Leave this place and go up to Judea, so that your followers will see the things you are doing. No one hides what he is doing if he is well known. Since you are doing these things, let the whole world know about you" (Jn 7:3–5).

Why waste your time in out-of-the-way Galilee, when you can be a worldwide celebrity. More than once, he must have said to Peter "Get behind me, Satan."

We're tempted too to give up our ideals or water them down because of what others think or say, or to fit in.

ST. PAUL OF THE CROSS

In his spiritual diary written early in his life while on retreat, St. Paul of the Cross describes a day when, after Holy Communion, he is *"filled with affliction and deep melancholy–also tempted with compassion for my family. Seeing people, hearing them pass, and the sound of bells irritated me"* (Spiritual Diary, November 25, 1720).

He's being pulled away from the dream God has given him; he's tempted to go home and join the crowd.

PRAYER

Lord Jesus,
"All these kingdoms will be yours, if . . ."
Were there days
when promises looked better broken;
right and truth only unreal dreams;
and life secure somewhere else?
We would rather see you strong
than hungry and weak.

Forty days alone,
no miracles, no eager crowds,
no friendly space to buoy you up,
no companion but the Evil One.

By the mystery of your temptation
in the desert,
Lord Jesus, have mercy on us.
Amen.

GOSPEL

JESUS SAID TO HIS DISCIPLES:

"When the Son of Man comes in his glory, and all the angels with him, he will sit upon his glorious throne, and all the nations will be assembled before him. And he will separate them one from another, as a shepherd separates the sheep from the goats. He will place the sheep on his right and the goats on his left. Then the king will say to those on his right, 'Come, you who are blessed by my Father. Inherit the kingdom prepared for you from the foundation of the world. For I was hungry and you gave me food, I was thirsty and you gave me drink, a stranger and you welcomed me, naked and you clothed me, ill and you cared for me, in prison and you visited me.' Then the righteous will answer him and say, 'Lord, when did we see you hungry and feed you, or thirsty and give you drink? When did we see you a stranger and welcome you, or naked and clothe you? When did we see you ill or in prison, and visit you?' And the king will say to them in reply, 'Amen, I say to you, whatever you did for one of these least brothers of mine, you did for me.' Then he will say to those on his left, 'Depart from me, you accursed, into the eternal fire prepared for the Devil and his angels. For I was hungry and you gave me no food, I was thirsty and you gave me no drink, a stranger and you gave me no welcome, naked and you gave me no clothing, ill and in prison, and you did not care for me.' Then they will answer and say, 'Lord, when did we see you hungry or thirsty or a stranger or naked or ill or in prison, and not minister to your needs?' He will answer them, 'Amen, I say to you, what you did not do for one of these least ones, you did not do for me.' And these will go off to eternal punishment, but the righteous to eternal life."

MATTHEW 25: 31-46

REFLECTION

Lent is indeed a time to search the scriptures to know Jesus Christ. He's there in the Gospels; his powerful deeds, his miracles, the story of his sufferings and death, his rising from the dead. Jesus reveals himself, in this graced time, as once he did to his disciples on the way to Emmaus: in the scriptures and in "the breaking of the bread."

Yet, today's powerful Gospel reminds us that Jesus reveals himself in another way—in those he describes as "the least:" the hungry, the thirsty, the naked, the stranger, the sick, the prisoner. He identifies himself with those in need.

We have to find him there. By caring for our neighbor in need, we not only see Jesus but are called into his kingdom. Still, how surprised are those who find him in this way: "When did we see you?" The least are hard to see. To Mother Teresa, the poor and the needy were always "Christ in disguise." You have to discover him there.

For St. Paul of the Cross the mystery of Jesus Christ is not something you know from a book, but through love, a love that embraces your neighbor, especially "the least."

ST. PAUL OF THE CROSS

Writing to his family, he says: *"Remember, you will never please God if you do not love one another. Let there never be any dissension among you, and, if ever any sharp words should pass among you, be quiet at once and do not keep on talking . . . So I repeat to you with Saint John: love one another, love one another, for in this is the love of God known. Show great love toward God's poor"* (Letter 12, February 21, 1722).

PRAYER

Lord Jesus Christ,
may I see you in my neighbor,
especially in those in need,
who seem so unlike you.
with little charm or response,
ungrateful for interest or care.
May I love you in my neighbor,
the neighbor hard to love
and find you in the least of them.
Amen.

GOSPEL

JESUS SAID TO HIS DISCIPLES:

"In praying, do not babble like the pagans, who think that they will be heard because of their many words. Do not be like them. Your Father knows what you need before you ask him.

"This is how you are to pray:

Our Father who art in heaven,
>   hallowed be thy name,
>   thy Kingdom come,
thy will be done,
>   on earth as it is in heaven.
Give us this day our daily bread;
and forgive us our trespasses,
>   as we forgive those who trespass against us;
and lead us not into temptation,
>   but deliver us from evil.

"If you forgive men their transgressions, your heavenly Father will forgive you. But if you do not forgive men, neither will your Father forgive your transgressions."

MATTHEW 6: 7-15

REFLECTION

One of the greatest gifts Jesus gives us is the gift of prayer. He not only prays for us, but teaches how to pray. Creatures of God, we search for our Creator. "Our hearts are restless till they rest in you." In the Lord's Prayer Jesus helps our restless searching with a prayer that is his own.

We pray as he prays. We approach the One whom Jesus knows intimately as his Father. Destined for his Kingdom, we pray that it may come. Called to be united with him, we ask that his will be done, on earth as it is in heaven.

The Lord's Prayer is our basic Christian prayer which we learn by heart. It appears everywhere in the Church's life: in liturgy and sacraments, in public and private prayer. We treasure it.

Yet, though we memorize the Lord's Prayer as a set formula, we shouldn't just repeat it mechanically and thoughtlessly. It's meant to awaken our faith and lead us into the mystery of God where words end.

When Moses approached God on Mount Sinai, a voice told him: "Do not come near; put off your shoes from your feet, for the place on which you are standing is holy ground." Jesus invites us to approach God, not as fearful strangers, but as children born of his grace.

St. Paul of the Cross saw prayer always leading to intimacy with God. It isn't just words. It leads to a Presence that words can't describe.

ST. PAUL OF THE CROSS

"Prayer is more perfect when it's interior, when a soul prays in the spirit of God. These are deep words, I know, but God can make even stones like me speak when he wishes. Let the Immense Good rest in your soul. God in you and you in God. A divine work. I don't know how to say it, but God feeds on your spirit and your spirit feeds on the Spirit of God. My food is Christ and I am his" (Letter 752, May 25, 1751).

PRAYER

"Lord, teach us to pray."
Give us, your children, the words to say,
tell us what they mean,
and make them lead to you.
Bring us as we pray
into that Presence within,
where words end
and where we rest in you.
Amen.

GOSPEL

While still more people gathered in the crowd, Jesus said to them, "This generation is an evil generation; it seeks a sign, but no sign will be given it, except the sign of Jonah. Just as Jonah became a sign to the Ninevites, so will the Son of Man be to this generation. At the judgment the queen of the south will rise with the men of this generation and she will condemn them, because she came from the ends of the earth to hear the wisdom of Solomon, and there is something greater than Solomon here. At the judgment the men of Nineveh will arise with this generation and condemn it, because at the preaching of Jonah they repented, and there is something greater than Jonah here."

LUKE 11: 29-32

REFLECTION

Jonah wasn't much of a sign himself, if you look at him. Frightened, he fled from a divine task to preach to the great city of Nineveh. When the sailors threw him from the boat because they thought he cursed their ship, he couldn't stop them. He would have been finished if the whale didn't swallow him and vomit him up on the shore at Nineveh.

An arrival like that caught the attention of the Ninevites. They would have ignored someone arriving by boat to their city. But who wouldn't listen to a man spewed out from the belly of a whale? Jonah was a blessed sign of life and they begged for God's forgiveness when he spoke.

In Jesus, a greater than Jonah is here. The mystery of his death and Resurrection is at the heart of his mission, his great word, his message of hope, his sign of love to us. We hear it during Lent and we should proclaim it to the world.

His promise of Resurrection and union with God was also at the heart of the message of St. Paul of the Cross. It's behind the smallest piece of advice he gives. In the mystery of his death and Resurrection Jesus, the Good Shepherd, leads us to the Father's Presence where death is no more and we have eternal life. Even now, we make that journey in prayer.

ST. PAUL OF THE CROSS

"Now when love leads you, you who are nothing, into his sheepfold, which is the bosom of the Eternal Father, shouldn't you obey? The gentle Jesus, speaking of his elect, says: 'Father, where I am I will my servant to be.' One remains in the bosom of the Father, and the soul united to him in pure and holy love stays there with him 'in the bosom of the Father' and there feeds on love, and love divinizes it" (Letter 1033, July 20, 1756).

PRAYER

Lord Jesus,
risen from the dead,
you are far greater than Jonah,
and you are here with us now.

I believe
you are our Resurrection and our life.
Give me a share of your risen life,
bring me to the place of your promise.
Stay with me and bring me home. Amen.

GOSPEL

JESUS SAID TO HIS DISCIPLES:

"Ask and it will be given to you; seek and you will find; knock and the door will be opened to you. For everyone who asks, receives; and the one who seeks, finds; and to the one who knocks, the door will be opened. Which one of you would hand his son a stone when he asked for a loaf of bread, or a snake when he asked for a fish? If you then, who are wicked, know how to give good gifts to your children, how much more will your heavenly Father give good things to those who ask him.

"Do to others whatever you would have them do to you. This is the law and the prophets."

MATTHEW 7: 7-12

REFLECTION

Does God answer prayers? A question often asked over the centuries. For some, God—if there is one—doesn't pay attention to us at all. We're on our own. No one's listening and no one cares.

Certainly, Jesus believed in a Father who cared; he asked for things in prayer from him and taught us to pray as he did. In the Garden of Gethsemane he asked over and over that his life be spared. "Father, let this cup pass from me." As he knocked the door opened, the answer came, yet not as he willed, but as God willed. To accept that answer "an angel came to strengthen him."

That experience of Jesus is a model for us as we pray for things. Ultimately, God gives good gifts to us his children, but according to his will; he knows what we need. He gave his only Son the gift of new life, though he had to first pass through death.

St. Paul of the Cross recognized the mystery surrounding petitionary prayer. Ultimately our prayer is answered, but often enough in mysterious ways we find hard to understand. Our faith is tested when we pray for things.

ST. PAUL OF THE CROSS

"I thank the Father of Mercies that you are improved in health, and you say well that the Lord seems to be playing games. That's what Scripture says: 'God plays on the earth,' and 'My delights are to be with the children of men.' How fortunate is the soul that silently in faith allows the games of love the Sovereign Good plays and abandons itself to his good pleasure, whether in health or sickness, in life or in death!" (Letter 920, September 3, 1754).

PRAYER

Lord,
I ask, I seek, I knock,
and wait for an answer to come.
Let me trust, not in my words,
or in my own desires,
or even the depth of my need,
but in your goodness and mercy.
Hear my prayer
and let it be done
according to your will.
Amen.

GOSPEL

JESUS SAID TO HIS DISCIPLES:

"I tell you, unless your righteousness surpasses that of the scribes and Pharisees, you will not enter into the Kingdom of heaven.

"You have heard that it was said to your ancestors, *You shall not kill; and whoever kills will be liable to judgment.* But I say to you, whoever is angry with his brother will be liable to judgment, and whoever says to his brother, *Raqa,* will be answerable to the Sanhedrin, and whoever says, 'You fool,' will be liable to fiery Gehenna. Therefore, if you bring your gift to the altar, and there recall that your brother has anything against you, leave your gift there at the altar, go first and be reconciled with your brother, and then come and offer your gift. Settle with your opponent quickly while on the way to court. Otherwise your opponent will hand you over to the judge, and the judge will hand you over to the guard, and you will be thrown into prison. Amen, I say to you, you will not be released until you have paid the last penny."

MATTHEW 5: 20-26

REFLECTION

Anger and harsh words don't seem to be the equivalent of murder, but Jesus seems to equate them in today's Gospel. They're all liable to judgment, he says.

We may dismiss his words as exaggerations, but before we do, think of instances you may know where people have been destroyed by words or angry rejection. It's not uncommon. Killing someone's spirit, taking away someone's reputation may not draw a jail sentence here on earth, but God sees the harm that's done. Often, so do we.

Murder takes away physical life, but we also must respect others as persons made in God's image. "Respect" is a wonderful word. It means "to look again" in Latin, to look again at someone and see a value we may have denied or missed, to constantly reassess how we judge another. Jesus says we should do this as we come before God's altar to offer our gift. It's one of the reasons behind the sign of peace we offer our neighbor at Mass.

As we look at another, we have to look honestly at ourselves too.

ST. PAUL OF THE CROSS

Respect is a form of love, *"love toward your neighbor, putting up with the faults of others, looking at all with charity and compassion, having a good opinion of everyone and a bad opinion only of yourself. A simple eye lets you see your neighbor as full of virtues and yourself full of vices, but without discouragement, peacefully, humbly"* (Letter 525, March 16, 1748).

PRAYER

Lord,
give me that second sight
that sees again
beyond the first angry word,
the first quick judgment,
the first souring assessment.
Give me that simple eye
that searches for the good
and patiently believes it will be there.
Give me eyes like yours.
Amen.

GOSPEL

JESUS SAID TO HIS DISCIPLES:

"You have heard that it was said, *You shall love your neighbor and hate your enemy.* But I say to you, love your enemies, and pray for those who persecute you, that you may be children of your heavenly Father, for he makes his sun rise on the bad and the good, and causes rain to fall on the just and the unjust. For if you love those who love you, what recompense will you have? Do not the tax collectors do the same? And if you greet your brothers and sisters only, what is unusual about that? Do not the pagans do the same? So be perfect, just as your heavenly Father is perfect."

MATTHEW 5: 43-48

REFLECTION

We pray often in the liturgy to grow in love, as individuals and as a church. From our earliest years we're meant to love more and more. Today's reading tells us we're to imitate our heavenly Father "who makes his sun rise on the bad and the good and causes rain to fall on the just and the unjust." We're called even to love our enemies.

Be careful, though, we're told from our earliest years. There are some people you can't trust; they'll take advantage of you; they'll do you harm. You have enemies in this world.

Jesus doesn't condemn reasonable caution; evil and evil people do exist. He had enemies; he was careful what he said to the scribes and authorities of his day. Rather, he's concerned about the pessimism that leads us to condemn someone or some groups absolutely. If we see no possible goodness or possible change in people, only intractable evil, then we don't see as God sees.

The sun of God's goodness shines on this world; the rain of his mercy softens its hardest places. His love changes people for the good.

But we can't just reason our way to a love like God's, St. Paul of the Cross taught, we grow to it through prayer, and so we need to rest in a loving God:

ST. PAUL OF THE CROSS

"So lose yourself completely in God, rest on his divine breast, adore him, love him, and, if you cannot say a word, that's even better. Remain continually in prayer, recollected in God. Love speaks little and expresses itself more in silence. One loving word is enough: 'Father! Great Father! Goodness! Love!' One word is enough to hold a loving soul for a long time in prayer" (Letter 1156, August 31, 1758).

PRAYER

Lord,
teach me the love you call me to,
the love sun-like, shining on all,
the love rain-like, falling on any ground,
looking for no response or return.
Show me the love
in the great word you spoke,
the dark word of your cross.
I learn love slowly, Lord,
teach me.
Amen.

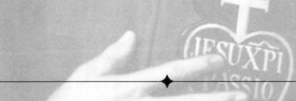

SECOND WEEK
OF
LENT

GOSPEL

Jesus took Peter, James, and John his brother, and led them up a high mountain by themselves. And he was transfigured before them; his face shone like the sun and his clothes became white as light. And behold, Moses and Elijah appeared to them, conversing with him. Then Peter said to Jesus in reply, "Lord, it is good that we are here. If you wish, I will make three tents here, one for you, one for Moses, and one for Elijah." While he was still speaking, behold, a bright cloud cast a shadow over them, then from the cloud came a voice that said, "This is my beloved Son, with whom I am well pleased; listen to him." When the disciples heard this, they fell prostrate and were very much afraid. But Jesus came and touched them, saying, "Rise, and do not be afraid." And when the disciples raised their eyes, they saw no one else but Jesus alone.

As they were coming down from the mountain, Jesus charged them, "Do not tell the vision to anyone until the Son of Man has been raised from the dead."

MATTHEW 17: 1-9

REFLECTION

The Transfiguration of Jesus takes place at the midpoint of Matthew's Gospel, after Jesus announces to his disciples that "he must go to Jerusalem and undergo great suffering at the hands of the elders and chief priests and scribes, and be killed, and on the third day be raised."

Take up your cross and follow me, he tells his disciples.

"God forbid, Lord," says Peter who doesn't understand this at all. We find it hard to understand too.

Six days later, Jesus takes Peter, James, and John up a mountain where they experience him glorified, surrounded by Moses and Elijah. It seems to be a transitory experience, one they can't prolong. After falling to the ground, they looked up and "saw no one except Jesus himself alone." But the experience strengthens them for the rest of the journey they make.

"The main purpose of the transfiguration was to remove the scandal of the cross from the hearts of Christ's disciples," says Pope Leo the Great.

What mountain does Jesus take us to strengthen us on our journey carrying our cross? St. Paul of the Cross and other spiritual guides say it's the mountain of prayer where we experience intimations of God's glory, brief encounters, and transfigurations of a lesser kind.

ST. PAUL OF THE CROSS

"Don't think that the trials and crosses you experience tell you to go another way. Trials don't indicate you're straying from God. We know it's just the opposite from the scriptures we read and the saints we honor. The way to go is the way our Savior gives us grace to go. Saint Bernard wasn't the first to know this truth when he cried out: 'The cross is the way to life, the way to glory, the way to the Kingdom, and the way to the inhabited City'" (Letter 1194, May 26, 1759).

PRAYER

Lord Jesus,
lead me to that mountain place
of stronger light and sure sound
where I may see your glory.

Light and truth,
bright as blinding snow,
whom Peter, James, and John saw,
"Bring me to your holy mountain,
to your dwelling place."
Amen.

GOSPEL

Jesus took Peter, James and John and led them up a high mountain apart by themselves. And he was transfigured before them, and his clothes became dazzling white, such as no fuller on earth could bleach them. Then Elijah appeared to them along with Moses, and they were conversing with Jesus. Then Peter said to Jesus in reply, "Rabbi, it is good that we are here! Let us make three tents: one for you, one for Moses, and one for Elijah." He hardly knew what to say, they were so terrified. Then a cloud came, casting a shadow over them; from the cloud came a voice, "This is my beloved Son. Listen to him." Suddenly, looking around, they no longer saw anyone but Jesus alone with them.

As they were coming down from the mountain, he charged them not to relate what they had seen to anyone, except when the Son of Man had risen from the dead. So they kept the matter to themselves, questioning what rising from the dead meant.

MARK 9: 2-10

REFLECTION

When Jesus was transfigured before the eyes of his disciples on the mountain, two figures converse with him: Elijah and Moses. What did they speak about?

Both of these great prophets were given a mission by God to free their people from slavery and they were persecuted and suffered for what they did. Certainly, they were reminders that a mission from God, however just and good it is, is always a call to sacrifice. It's the prophets' destiny and the destiny of the church.

But the prophets also point to God's eternal, steady plan for the salvation of the whole world. On the way to Emmaus after his Resurrection, two of Jesus' disciples voice disappointment about his death; Jesus replies that the prophets declared that "the Messiah should suffer all these things and enter into his glory." His glorious Resurrection is a sign that God's plan for the salvation of the world is fulfilled.

A mountain is a place for seeing far and wide. On the mountain of the Transfiguration, Jesus glorified reveals God's plan for saving the world. "This is my Son, my beloved, listen to him," God says. "It is good to be here," the disciples say. The mystery of the Transfiguration anticipates in a transitory way the promise of God's kingdom. It will come.

Is prayer the mountain where we anticipate this promised union with God? St. Paul of the Cross thought so:

ST. PAUL OF THE CROSS

"Lucy, God wishes to make you holy. Be humble of heart and continue your prayer in God, the prayer God gives you. . . . Die that mystical death to all that is not God . . . Lucy ought not to be living in herself, but in God. Jesus lives in Lucy and Lucy in Jesus. Tell me: Is this the way it is going? If it goes so, it goes well! (Letter 752, May 25, 1751).

PRAYER

Lord Jesus,
lead me to that mountain close by,
within,
that I can climb each day;
the holy ground I stand on
now.
Amen.

GOSPEL

Jesus took Peter, John, and James and went up the mountain to pray. While he was praying his face changed in appearance and his clothing became dazzling white. And behold, two men were conversing with him, Moses and Elijah, who appeared in glory and spoke of his exodus that he was going to accomplish in Jerusalem. Peter and his companions had been overcome by sleep, but becoming fully awake, they saw his glory and the two men standing with him. As they were about to part from him, Peter said to Jesus, "Master, it is good that we are here; let us make three tents, one for you, one for Moses, and one for Elijah." But he did not know what he was saying. While he was still speaking, a cloud came and cast a shadow over them, and they became frightened when they entered the cloud. Then from the cloud came a voice that said, "This is my chosen Son; listen to him." After the voice had spoken, Jesus was found alone. They fell silent and did not at that time tell anyone what they had seen.

LUKE 9: 28B-36

REFLECTION

Luke's Gospel is the only one that says explicitly that Jesus and his disciples "went up onto the mountain to pray." Prayer opens the way to great mysteries, according to Luke.

"While Jesus is praying" his face is changed in appearance, his clothes become dazzlingly white and Moses and Elijah talk with him. He also sees Moses and Elijah appearing in glory speaking of "his passage which he is about to fulfill in Jerusalem."

Luke's account anticipates the later Emmaus story when the risen Jesus recalls to his disciples on the road what the prophets said of his death and Resurrection, his passage into glory.

66

But it's prayer that the evangelist wants us mostly to remember. Prayer gives us the gift to see things from God's perspective rather than from our own. As Jesus and his disciples prayed on the mountain, human reason and experience bowed before a greater light and power. After falling "into a deep sleep" the disciples briefly experience God's glory before they continue on their journey to Jerusalem.

As he guided people in prayer, St. Paul of the Cross told them to pray faithfully and regularly. Moments of transfiguration were waiting. The Holy Spirit was calling them to a high place to meet God.

ST. PAUL OF THE CROSS

"Prayer is not to be made according to our ideas, but directed by the Holy Spirit. It's best to begin your prayer on the mysteries of the holy Passion, for that is the gateway. 'I am the door, and no one comes to the Father except through me.' But when the soul gets lost in the immensity of the Divinity and caught in the vision of the Infinite Good in faith and fed by love, it should remain that way. It would be a serious mistake to turn away to anything else" (Letter 764, July 20, 1751).

PRAYER

> Lord Jesus,
> lead me to that mountain,
> that bright mountain
> "where God instructs us in his ways
> that we may walk in his truth."
> Teach me to pray
> and to rest there.
> Amen.

GOSPEL

JESUS SAID TO HIS DISCIPLES:

"Be merciful, just as your Father is merciful.

"Stop judging and you will not be judged. Stop condemning and you will not be condemned. Forgive and you will be forgiven. Give and gifts will be given to you; a good measure, packed together, shaken down, and overflowing, will be poured into your lap. For the measure with which you measure will in return be measured out to you."

LUKE 6: 36-38

REFLECTION

In Matthew's Gospel Jesus teaches his disciples on a mountain. In Luke's Gospel, read today, Jesus prays on the mountain then descends to teach his disciples about loving others, especially one's enemies. He explores the meaning of the beatitude "Blessed are the merciful for they shall obtain mercy."

Mercy goes beyond not judging, not condemning, just forgiving, he says. It gives gifts to others, like the merciful father of the prodigal son whom Luke will describe later. The father offers his ungrateful son a feast of unearned graces—"bring a robe—the best one—and put it on him, put a ring on his finger and sandals on his feet." God's mercy isn't measured or cautious or bound by recrimination.

Feuds, quarrels and vendettas were common in the small wary towns of the Tuscan Maremma where Paul of the Cross preached missions. Poverty, which was pervasive in that area, had a way of making people quarrelsome. It's said that often Paul would carry a cross into a deeply divided home and beg family members to forgive one another or their enemies next door in the name of Jesus Christ. His efforts sometimes succeeded.

In religious communities too he often spoke of mercy:

ST. PAUL OF THE CROSS

"Learn how to excuse your sister and speak kindly to her. . . . See her in the Side of Jesus Christ and then you will love her with a pure and holy love. If she comes into the room, don't show annoyance, but put up with her and then remain recollected in God in holy silence" (Letter 67 December 14, 1733).

PRAYER

Lord,
let me see in myself
the same human frailty, selfishness and sinfulness that I see in others.
Teach me to be merciful
with the mercy that I see in you.
Amen.

GOSPEL

Jesus spoke to the crowds and to his disciples, saying, "The scribes and the Pharisees have taken their seat on the chair of Moses. Therefore, do and observe all things whatsoever they tell you, but do not follow their example. For they preach but they do not practice. They tie up heavy burdens hard to carry and lay them on people's shoulders, but they will not lift a finger to move them. All their works are performed to be seen. They widen their phylacteries and lengthen their tassels. They love places of honor at banquets, seats of honor in synagogues, greetings in marketplaces, and the salutation 'Rabbi.' As for you, do not be called 'Rabbi.' You have but one teacher, and you are all brothers. Call no one on earth your father; you have but one Father in heaven. Do not be called 'Master'; you have but one master, the Christ. The greatest among you must be your servant. Whoever exalts himself will be humbled; but whoever humbles himself will be exalted."

MATTHEW 23: 1-12

REFLECTION

The nineteenth century British historian, Lord Acton said "Power tends to corrupt, and absolute power corrupts absolutely." He was speaking about the tendency in all societies for those in power to use it for themselves and their own aims.

Jesus' words to his disciples describe the Jewish power structure of his day. The original readers of Matthew's Gospel, probably written in Palestine or Syria towards the end of the first century, knew well the Jewish communities around them. They would see abuses of power in them, but more importantly would they see it in their own church and in themselves too?

Abuse of power is usually there no matter what society, secular or religious, you consider, and it's found on many levels.

St. Paul of the Cross was no modern social critic and had no grand prescriptions for reforming the government or the church of his day. But he did see temptations of power in ordinary people with authority over others, like Thomas Fossi whom he directed many years. Fossi, a married man with a successful business tended to try to run other people's lives, especially his own family's life.

Paul also saw the dangers of power-seeking in himself and he offers himself to Fossi as an example:

ST. PAUL OF THE CROSS

"You make me laugh . . . saying that you want me to take charge of you. You don't even know me. I don't want to be in charge of anyone, nor have I ever thought of being a director, neither yours or anyone else's. If I thought I knew how to direct others, I would be a devil in the flesh. God deliver me from it . . . I want to serve everyone and to offer some holy advice, based on holy truth and on what the spiritual masters say—to anyone who asks it of me" (Letter 863, August 14,1753).

PRAYER

Lord,
it's easy to see the faults of others,
and prescribe a remedy for them.
Harder to see faults of our own;
and recognize the wrong we have done.

Give me grace to serve
and not be served.
Give us a world that serves even the least.
Amen.

GOSPEL

As Jesus was going up to Jerusalem, he took the Twelve disciples aside by themselves, and said to them on the way, "Behold, we are going up to Jerusalem, and the Son of Man will be handed over to the chief priests and the scribes, and they will condemn him to death, and hand him over to the Gentiles to be mocked and scourged and crucified, and he will be raised on the third day."

Then the mother of the sons of Zebedee approached Jesus with her sons and did him homage, wishing to ask him for something. He said to her, "What do you wish?" She answered him, "Command that these two sons of mine sit, one at your right and the other at your left, in your kingdom." Jesus said in reply, "You do not know what you are asking. Can you drink the chalice that I am going to drink?" They said to him, "We can." He replied, "My chalice you will indeed drink, but to sit at my right and at my left, this is not mine to give but is for those for whom it has been prepared by my Father." When the ten heard this, they became indignant at the two brothers. But Jesus summoned them and said, "You know that the rulers of the Gentiles lord it over them, and the great ones make their authority over them felt. But it shall not be so among you. Rather, whoever wishes to be great among you shall be your servant; whoever wishes to be first among you shall be your slave. Just so, the Son of Man did not come to be served but to serve and to give his life as a ransom for many."

MATTHEW 20: 17-28

REFLECTION

We usually think that Lent is a personal journey, but that's not all it is. Lent is a time for the whole church to be renewed.

"We" are going up to Jerusalem, Jesus says to his disciples in Matthew's Gospel and they follow him to the holy place of challenge and reward, to be renewed by the graces of his paschal mystery.

On the journey, the mother James and John saw an opportunity for herself and them. "Command that these two sons of mine sit, one at your right and the other at your left, in your kingdom." She's looking for power and prestige.

Jesus reminds her that his followers are not to be served, but to serve. It will cost them and not make them rich, for "the Son of Man did not come to be served but to serve and to give his life as a ransom for many."

The mother's request for power won't be the last request of that kind from disciples of Jesus. It's a temptation most of us share. The Church has always been beset by members using its resources and power for themselves. That's why Jesus' words are so important to hear during Lent. Service of others is a good part of the cross we should bear.

Writing to his brothers and sisters after his mother's death, Paul of the Cross urged them to love and serve one another:

ST. PAUL OF THE CROSS

"Obey one another, especially the younger toward the older although with you there should be no seniority. Be humble, wait upon one another, console one another. I particularly recommend that you respect your sisters much, showing them all possible deference, treating them charitably, and assisting them in all their needs" (Letter 12, February 21, 1722).

PRAYER

At the table of life,
let me be me one who serves,
like you, O Lord.
let me bend down to wash the feet of others;
let me give life to them,
like you, O Lord.
Amen.

GOSPEL

JESUS SAID TO THE PHARISEES:

"There was a rich man who dressed in purple garments and fine linen and dined sumptuously each day. And lying at his door was a poor man named Lazarus, covered with sores, who would gladly have eaten his fill of the scraps that fell from the rich man's table. Dogs even used to come and lick his sores. When the poor man died, he was carried away by angels to the bosom of Abraham. The rich man also died and was buried, and from the netherworld, where he was in torment, he raised his eyes and saw Abraham far off and Lazarus at his side. And he cried out, 'Father Abraham, have pity on me. Send Lazarus to dip the tip of his finger in water and cool my tongue, for I am suffering torment in these flames.' Abraham replied, 'My child, remember that you received what was good during your lifetime while Lazarus likewise received what was bad; but now he is comforted here, whereas you are tormented. Moreover, between us and you a great chasm is established to prevent anyone from crossing who might wish to go from our side to yours or from your side to ours.' He said, 'Then I beg you, father, send him to my father's house, for I have five brothers, so that he may warn them, lest they too come to this place of torment.' But Abraham replied, 'They have Moses and the prophets. Let them listen to them.' He said, 'Oh no, father Abraham, but if someone from the dead goes to them, they will repent.' Then Abraham said, 'If they will not listen to Moses and the prophets, neither will they be persuaded if someone should rise from the dead.'"

LUKE 16: 19-31

REFLECTION

The rich man in this parable is so absorbed in himself and his "good" life that he sees nothing else, not the poor man at his door nor his own inevitable death. The scriptures often speak of that same kind of blindness: "In his riches, man lacks wisdom; he is like the beasts that are destroyed" (Psalm 49).

The warning is not just for the rich, however. The same psalm calls for "people both high and low, rich and poor alike" to listen. A small store of talents and gifts can be just as absorbing and make us just as shortsighted as a great store of riches. Whether we have much or little, we can be blind to the poor at our gate.

We're destined for a life beyond this one and what we do and how we live here will count there. A judgment is coming.

Jesus' parable offers another reminder. Even if someone returns from the dead, even if Jesus rises from the dead, some will not believe. In him, God offers a share in his risen life. A great gift has been given, but like the sign of Jonah, some will not believe.

One way to adjust our way of thinking is prayer. Our blindness comes because we only see what's before our eyes. Look at God's gifts in prayer, St. Paul of the Cross writes, and everything else becomes nothing.

ST. PAUL OF THE CROSS

"Who wouldn't love our Father of Mercies, who invites us so kindly and draws us so sweetly? Let us run, let us run, Signora, after the One who loves us, casting ourselves completely on the bosom of his love. Let no difficulty frighten us, or daily faults, or miseries, for these only bring us to the throne of his mercies. If he hides, it's so that we may humble ourselves and look for shelter in the shadow of his wings, and then he will show us his face and gladden our hearts by his love." (Letter 29, April 15, 1727)

PRAYER

Lord, source of all good,
good beyond what we have or can see,
give me wisdom to know you and your gifts
to see as you see and love as you love.
Like the blind man, I want to see.
Amen.

GOSPEL

JESUS SAID TO THE CHIEF PRIESTS AND THE ELDERS OF THE PEOPLE:

"Hear another parable. There was a landowner who planted a vineyard, put a hedge around it, dug a wine press in it, and built a tower. Then he leased it to tenants and went on a journey. When vintage time drew near, he sent his servants to the tenants to obtain his produce. But the tenants seized the servants and one they beat, another they killed, and a third they stoned. Again he sent other servants, more numerous than the first ones, but they treated them in the same way. Finally, he sent his son to them, thinking, 'They will respect my son.' But when the tenants saw the son, they said to one another, 'This is the heir. Come, let us kill him and acquire his inheritance.' They seized him, threw him out of the vineyard, and killed him. What will the owner of the vineyard do to those tenants when he comes?" They answered him, "He will put those wretched men to a wretched death and lease his vineyard to other tenants who will give him the produce at the proper times." Jesus said to them, "Did you never read in the Scriptures:

The stone that the builders rejected
has become the cornerstone;
by the Lord has this been done,
and it is wonderful in our eyes?

Therefore, I say to you, the Kingdom of God will be taken away from you and given to a people that will produce its fruit." When the chief priests and the Pharisees heard his parables, they knew that he was speaking about them. And although they were attempting to arrest him, they feared the crowds, for they regarded him as a prophet.

MATTHEW 21: 33-43, 45-46

REFLECTION

As Jesus entered Jerusalem before his death, a large crowd acclaimed him as "the prophet Jesus from Nazareth in Galilee" and spread their cloaks and branches before him. "Hosanna to the Son of David. Blessed is he who comes in the name of the Lord."

Going into the temple, he drives out those who were buying and selling there, a symbolic act that restores it as a place of prayer. (Matthew 21:1–18) The Jewish leaders react strongly, asking by what authority he does these things. In response, Jesus accepts the people's testimony—he is the Son of David, sent by God. Their leaders will reject him, as others have rejected the prophets before him, and will put him to death.

Conviction about his mission—that "the stone rejected by the builders will become the cornerstone"—does not insulate Jesus from the pain of rejection, however. He suffers from it as the prophets before him did, and his suffering is increased as the acclaiming crowds fall silent and his own disciples abandon him.

One of Jesus' greatest sufferings was rejection by his own.

Like so many founders of religious orders, Paul of the Cross suffered from forms of rejection: uncertainty, misunderstanding, and lack of support and the grinding slowness of a Church that had so many other things to do. He was not always a patient prophet.

ST. PAUL OF THE CROSS

"I am always more miserable, assaulted by demons and by men, scourged with their tongues, with calumnies of others, besides my struggles within. Oh, how much I need the assistance of God and of prayers.

"On Monday I leave for Rome, and I am going into battle to answer to points of the Constitutions and to overcome so many contradictions and difficulties" (Letter 132, January 24, 1737).

PRAYER

Lord,
how often we reject you when we reject others,
when we ignore their truth, their vision, their cries for justice.
Help us hear the prophets and their message,
not just the prophets of old,
but the prophets at our side.
Amen.

GOSPEL

Tax collectors and sinners were all drawing near to listen to Jesus, but the Pharisees and scribes began to complain, saying, "This man welcomes sinners and eats with them." So to them Jesus addressed this parable. "A man had two sons, and the younger son said to his father, 'Father, give me the share of your estate that should come to me.' So the father divided the property between them. After a few days, the younger son collected all his belongings and set off to a distant country where he squandered his inheritance on a life of dissipation. When he had freely spent everything, a severe famine struck that country, and he found himself in dire need. So he hired himself out to one of the local citizens who sent him to his farm to tend the swine. And he longed to eat his fill of the pods on which the swine fed, but nobody gave him any. Coming to his senses he thought, 'How many of my father's hired workers have more than enough food to eat, but here am I, dying from hunger. I shall get up and go to my father and I shall say to him, "Father, I have sinned against heaven and against you. I no longer deserve to be called your son; treat me as you would treat one of your hired workers."' So he got up and went back to his father. While he was still a long way off, his father caught sight of him, and was filled with compassion. He ran to his son, embraced him and kissed him. His son said to him, 'Father, I have sinned against heaven and against you; I no longer deserve to be called your son.' But his father ordered his servants, 'Quickly, bring the finest robe and put it on him; put a ring on his finger and sandals on his feet. Take the fattened calf and slaughter it. Then let us celebrate with a feast, because this son of mine was dead, and has come to life again; he was lost, and has been found.' Then the celebration began. Now the older son had been out in the field and, on his way back, as he neared the house, he heard the sound of music and dancing. He called one of the servants and asked what this might mean. The servant said to him, 'Your brother has returned and your father has slaughtered the fattened calf because he has him back safe and sound.' He became angry, and when he refused to enter the house, his father came out and pleaded with him. He said to his father in reply, 'Look, all these years I served you and not once did I disobey your orders; yet you never gave me even a young goat to feast on with my friends. But when your son returns who swallowed up your property with prostitutes, for him you slaughter the fattened calf.' He said to him, 'My son, you are here with me always; everything I have is yours. But now we must celebrate and rejoice, because your brother was dead and has come to life again; he was lost and has been found.'"

LUKE 15: 1-3, 11-32

REFLECTION

The story of the prodigal son is not just about a boy gone astray; it's about the human race gone wrong.

"Give me what's mine," the son says boldly to his father, and he takes off for a faraway country, that permissive paradise that promises power and pleasure—in fact, everything. They're empty promises, of course, and soon the boy who had so much has nothing and ends up in a pigsty feeding pigs who eat better than he does.

Then, he takes his first step back. He "comes to himself," our story says; he realizes what he has done. "I have sinned."

How straightforward his reaction! Not blaming anybody else for the mess he's in: not his father, or the prostitutes, or society that took him in. No, it's his own fault. He doesn't wallow in his sin, either. He looks to the place where he belongs, to his father's house. It won't be an easy road, but he takes it. He starts back home.

Like so many of the saints, Paul of the Cross saw himself for all his holiness as a prodigal son, undeserving of God and a place at his side.

ST. PAUL OF THE CROSS

He is *"plunged in the depths of misery. . . . My sins deserve this. . . . Recommend my soul to God"* (Letter 26, December 23, 1734).

He's not exaggerating. If the prodigal son is an image of the human race, then we're all making the journey home with him.

PRAYER

How easily we leave your side,
Lord God,
for a place far away.
Send light into our darkness,
and open our eyes to our sins.
Unless you give us new hearts and strong spirits,
we cannot make the journey home
to your welcoming arms and the music and the dancing.
Amen.

THIRD WEEK
OF
LENT

GOSPEL

Jesus came to a town of Samaria called Sychar, near the plot of land that Jacob had given to his son Joseph. Jacob's well was there. Jesus, tired from his journey, sat down there at the well. It was about noon.

A woman of Samaria came to draw water. Jesus said to her, "Give me a drink." His disciples had gone into the town to buy food. The Samaritan woman said to him, "How can you, a Jew, ask me, a Samaritan woman, for a drink?" — For Jews use nothing in common with Samaritans. — Jesus answered and said to her, "If you knew the gift of God and who is saying to you, 'Give me a drink,' you would have asked him and he would have given you living water." The woman said to him, "Sir, you do not even have a bucket and the cistern is deep; where then can you get this living water? Are you greater than our father Jacob, who gave us this cistern and drank from it himself with his children and his flocks?" Jesus answered and said to her, "Everyone who drinks this water will be thirsty again; but whoever drinks the water I shall give will never thirst; the water I shall give will become in him a spring of water welling up to eternal life." The woman said to him, "Sir, give me this water, so that I may not be thirsty or have to keep coming here to draw water."

Jesus said to her, "Go call your husband and come back." The woman answered and said to him, "I do not have a husband." Jesus answered her, "You are right in saying, 'I do not have a husband.' For you have had five husbands, and the one you have now is not your husband. What you have said is true." The woman said to him, "Sir, I can see that you are a prophet. Our ancestors worshiped on this mountain; but you people say that the place to worship is in Jerusalem." Jesus said to her, "Believe me, woman, the hour is coming when you will worship the Father neither on this mountain nor in Jerusalem. You people worship what you do not understand; we worship what we understand, because salvation is from the Jews. But the hour is coming, and is now here, when true worshipers will worship the Father in Spirit and truth; and indeed the

Father seeks such people to worship him. God is Spirit, and those who worship him must worship in Spirit and truth." The woman said to him, "I know that the Messiah is coming, the one called the Christ; when he comes, he will tell us everything." Jesus said to her, "I am he, the one speaking with you."

At that moment his disciples returned, and were amazed that he was talking with a woman, but still no one said, "What are you looking for?" or "Why are you talking with her?" The woman left her water jar and went into the town and said to the people, "Come see a man who told me everything I have done. Could he possibly be the Christ?" They went out of the town and came to him. Meanwhile, the disciples urged him, "Rabbi, eat." But he said to them, "I have food to eat of which you do not know." So the disciples said to one another, "Could someone have brought him something to eat?" Jesus said to them, "My food is to do the will of the one who sent me and to finish his work. Do you not say, 'In four months the harvest will be here'? I tell you, look up and see the fields ripe for the harvest. The reaper is already receiving payment and gathering crops for eternal life, so that the sower and reaper can rejoice together. For here the saying is verified that 'One sows and another reaps.' I sent you to reap what you have not worked for; others have done the work, and you are sharing the fruits of their work."

Many of the Samaritans of that town began to believe in him because of the word of the woman who testified, "He told me everything I have done." When the Samaritans came to him, they invited him to stay with them; and he stayed there two days. Many more began to believe in him because of his word, and they said to the woman, "We no longer believe because of your word; for we have heard for ourselves, and we know that this is truly the savior of the world."

JOHN 4: 5-42

Shorter form: JOHN 4:5-15, 19b-26, 39a, 40-42
Longer form may be optionally read on any day in the third week of Lent

REFLECTION

John's Gospel says that Jesus, setting out from Jerusalem for his native Galilee, "had" to pass through Samaria and meet the Samaritan woman at Jacob's well. So it was not by chance that Jesus, the Savior, enter that land whose people were so bitterly opposed to their neighbors, the Jews of Judea and Galilee.

"It was about noon, and Jesus, tired after his journey, was sitting by the well." A Samaritan woman came to the well for water. What a strong, unconventional woman she was! She came alone at noon, not the usual morning or evening time when women of the town came in groups with their water jars. Nor does she hesitate at the sight of a man sitting alone at the well.

How forceful and sarcastic her answer when Jesus asks for a drink! "What! You a Jew, ask for a drink from a Samaritan woman?" The ancient feud between Jews and Samaritans rises in her blood.

Yet the weary man persists, talking of human thirst and the living waters God provides. Gradually, as he talks of higher things, the woman recognizes he has more to give than water from the well; he fulfills all the memories associated with this ancient sacred place. He says something, however, she would rather not hear. "You have had five husbands, the man you are living with now is not your husband."

She must have heard it less as an accusation than as the truth, for she doesn't turn away. More than accusing her, she felt him refreshing her soul's thirst. Eager and inspired, she put down her water jar and hurried to the town to tell her neighbors about the one she met. For two days Jesus stayed in that town. The tired gentle Jew, who sat by Jacob's well, was welcomed as a Savior.

We must welcome him too; he comes to us and never tires of us.

ST. PAUL OF THE CROSS

"Feed yourself on Jesus, drink his Precious Blood, quench your thirst from the chalice of Jesus. Yet, the more you drink, the more you will thirst" (Letter 662, August 9, 1749).

PRAYER

O Jesus,
is the woman,
sure and strong,
our reflection:
sure but unsure,
strong but so weak,
seeking but afraid to find
our Savior so close by?
Amen.

GOSPEL

Since the Passover of the Jews was near, Jesus went up to Jerusalem. He found in the temple area those who sold oxen, sheep and doves, as well as the money changers seated there. He made a whip out of cords and drove them all out of the temple area, with sheep and oxen, and spilled the coins of the money changers and overturned their tables, and to those who sold doves he said, "Take these out of here, and stop making my Father's house a marketplace." His disciples recalled the words of Scripture, *Zeal for your house will consume me.* At this the Jews answered and said to him, "What sign can you show us for doing this?" Jesus answered and said to them, "Destroy this temple and in three days I will raise it up." The Jews said, "This temple has been under construction for forty-six years, and you will raise it up in three days?" But he was speaking about the temple of his body. Therefore, when he was raised from the dead, his disciples remembered that he had said this, and they came to believe the Scripture and the word Jesus had spoken.

While he was in Jerusalem for the feast of Passover, many began to believe in his name when they saw the signs he was doing. But Jesus would not trust himself to them because he knew them all, and did not need anyone to testify about human nature. He himself understood it well.

JOHN 2: 13-25

REFLECTION

Unlike the other Gospels that place Jesus' cleansing of the temple in Jerusalem close to his passion and death, John's Gospel puts it at the beginning of his ministry to show that opposition to him at the highest levels began early on. If he overturned the tables in the entranceway of the temple, what would he do next? Destroy it? Alarmed, the city's leaders kept a close watch on the Galilean trouble-maker.

The temple's history as the center of Jewish life and worship began with the first temple built by King Solomon. It was a sign of God's presence among his people.

Yet, as Jesus said to the Samaritan woman, the temple was a provisional place, as all earthly places are. It was destroyed by the Romans in 70 AD. Now, he was the new temple, the new lawgiver, the Word dwelling among us.

We still feel our faith shaken today when sacred places, institutions and familiar spiritual structures are destroyed or altered by change. Is God still with us, we ask? We need a deeper belief in God's abiding presence. The great gift of mystics like St. Paul of the Cross is their insistence that God dwells within us, even when outward signs disappear.

ST. PAUL OF THE CROSS

"Faith says that those who wait on the Lord will not be disappointed. 'Wait on the Lord and act bravely.' The way of the saints is to wait on the Lord in all trials and let our resistant nature die in the Divine Will. Mariana must die mystically, and that dying is not once. We must wait patiently through life for our Lord to visit. God is pleased with hope that endures suffering." (Letter 1765, December 28, 1768)

PRAYER

Once you came into the temple,
not to destroy it, but to build it anew.
come to us, Lord Jesus, and make us temples of God.
Cleanse us from all that is unholy.
Cleanse our church from its unholiness.
Cleanse our world and make it holy.
Amen.

GOSPEL

Some people told Jesus about the Galileans whose blood Pilate had mingled with the blood of their sacrifices. Jesus said to them in reply, "Do you think that because these Galileans suffered in this way they were greater sinners than all other Galileans? By no means! But I tell you, if you do not repent, you will all perish as they did! Or those eighteen people who were killed when the tower at Siloam fell on them – do you think they were more guilty than everyone else who lived in Jerusalem? By no means! But I tell you, if you do not repent, you will all perish as they did!"

And he told them this parable: "There once was a person who had a fig tree planted in his orchard, and when he came in search of fruit on it but found none, he said to the gardener, 'For three years now I have come in search of fruit on this fig tree but have found none. So cut it down. Why should it exhaust the soil?' He said to him in reply, 'Sir, leave it for this year also, and I shall cultivate the ground around it and fertilize it; it may bear fruit in the future. If not you can cut it down.'"

LUKE 13: 1-9

REFLECTION

Some of the hardest questions we ask about God are found already in the scriptures. For example, is God using tragedies like earthquakes and other natural disasters or accidents or random acts of violence to punish us? Or is it that he doesn't care?

That's the question posed to Jesus in today's Gospel: Why were eighteen people killed when a tower fell on them in Siloam; Why were people allowed to die in a sudden riot that the Roman procurator Pontius Pilate put down by slaughtering everyone in sight?

God's not punishing those involved in those tragedies, Jesus replied. Tragedies are part of life; they're sharp reminders that life on earth isn't permanent or without risk. They're calling us as Jesus called out to the barren fig tree: Be fruitful, the time is short.

In the winter of 1755, the superior of a convent of nuns wrote Paul of the Cross about a recent tragedy that had occurred: six of her sisters had just died. Was God displeased with her convent? Paul had just seen six of his own religious leave his small, infant congregation. Was God displeased with him?

ST. PAUL OF THE CROSS

"I keenly feel your pain," he writes, *"and I will not fail to pray, and have my religious pray, that the Lord will comfort you by having this merciful punishment cease. I have strong faith that the great Father of Mercies will turn this event to your spiritual advantage. So, I pray that you and all your good religious find comfort by uniting themselves with the adorable Divine Will that can only wish the greatest good"* (Letter 937, January 28, 1755).

Paul urged the sisters to look with "eyes of faith" on these deaths and to recognize "the Divine Pleasure." God's plan for the greatest good included the death of his only Son. It was not a punishment; the grain of wheat fell to the ground "to bear much fruit."

PRAYER

Lord, give me eyes of faith,
especially when the grain of wheat
falls to the ground and dies.
Then, I need other eyes
to see beyond the dead ground.
Give me eyes of faith.
Amen.

GOSPEL

JESUS SAID TO THE PEOPLE IN THE SYNAGOGUE AT NAZARETH:

"Amen, I say to you, no prophet is accepted in his own native place. Indeed, I tell you, there were many widows in Israel in the days of Elijah when the sky was closed for three and a half years and a severe famine spread over the entire land. It was to none of these that Elijah was sent, but only to a widow in Zarephath in the land of Sidon. Again, there were many lepers in Israel during the time of Elisha the prophet; yet not one of them was cleansed, but only Naaman the Syrian." When the people in the synagogue heard this, they were all filled with fury. They rose up, drove him out of the town, and led him to the brow of the hill on which their town had been built, to hurl him down headlong. But he passed through the midst of them and went away.

LUKE 4: 24-30

REFLECTION

Luke's Gospel brings us back to Nazareth, where Jesus lived most of his life among "his own." But his own reject him at the beginning of his ministry in their synagogue. Their rejection surely hurt him; how could he forget it?

The crowds that welcome him to Jerusalem on Palm Sunday call him "the prophet Jesus from Nazareth in Galilee." Yet so few disciples from Nazareth follow him; only a few women from there will stand by his cross as he dies. From what we know of Nazareth, Jesus did not find much acceptance there. "He came to his own and his own received him not."

The Lenten Gospels prepare us for the great mystery of Jesus' death and Resurrection by presenting him as one who took on himself our sorrows. They place before us the physical sorrows that come from the nails, the thorns, the scourging. But also there is the interior sorrow that rejection brought to him. Rejection by our own, someone close to us, will be one of the ways we share in the passion of Christ.

St. Paul of the Cross knew rejection by his own. His dream of a new religious community was initially rejected by the church at the highest levels; for much of his life people in the church opposed his plans. Only inner conviction kept him pursuing what he believed was God's Will.

That experience helped Paul encourage others who felt rejected, by God, or by those close to them, or by the adversities of life. It was a form of temptation, an interior cross that could lead to crushed dreams and disappointment, he said. Instead, look to the example of Jesus; he lifts us up.

ST. PAUL OF THE CROSS

"The ship is battered by storms and winds, but this only makes the power and wisdom of the Great Pilot, Jesus Christ, shine forth. May Jesus Christ live forever, for he gives us the strength to suffer every hardship for love of him. The works of God are always under attack so that the Divine Magnificence may shine forth. When everything crashes to the earth, that is when they can be seen to rise to the heights. 'The Lord slays and brings to life, brings them to Sheol and back again'" (Letter 47, November 29, 1730).

PRAYER

My God, I trust in you;
you're my guide, my help, my salvation.
When all seems lost
I am safely in your hands,
no evil can touch me.
Amen.

GOSPEL

Peter approached Jesus and asked him, "Lord, if my brother sins against me, how often must I forgive him? As many as seven times?" Jesus answered, "I say to you, not seven times but seventy-seven times. That is why the Kingdom of heaven may be likened to a king who decided to settle accounts with his servants. When he began the accounting, a debtor was brought before him who owed him a huge amount. Since he had no way of paying it back, his master ordered him to be sold, along with his wife, his children, and all his property, in payment of the debt. At that, the servant fell down, did him homage, and said, 'Be patient with me, and I will pay you back in full.' Moved with compassion the master of that servant let him go and forgave him the loan. When that servant had left, he found one of his fellow servants who owed him a much smaller amount. He seized him and started to choke him, demanding, 'Pay back what you owe.' Falling to his knees, his fellow servant begged him, 'Be patient with me, and I will pay you back.' But he refused. Instead, he had him put in prison until he paid back the debt. Now when his fellow servants saw what had happened, they were deeply disturbed, and went to their master and reported the whole affair. His master summoned him and said to him, 'You wicked servant! I forgave you your entire debt because you begged me to. Should you not have had pity on your fellow servant, as I had pity on you?' Then in anger his master handed him over to the torturers until he should pay back the whole debt. So will my heavenly Father do to you, unless each of you forgives your brother from your heart."

MATTHEW 18: 21-35

REFLECTION

Peter's question about forgiveness ("How many times must I forgive my brother?") isn't just his question. It's a question all of us ask.

Jesus answers that we should forgive as God forgives—beyond measure, and he offers a parable about two servants who owe money, a big reason people fight among themselves. The first of the servants owes his master five thousand talents, a huge sum, and in an unexpected display of mercy, his master forgives the entire debt.

After being forgiven so much, however, that servant sends off to debtors' prison another servant who owes him a few denarii, a mere pittance compared to his debt of ten thousand talents. He won't forgive this small thing.

Often enough, isn't the reason we don't forgive others just as small? So many grievances and grudges people have against one another are based on small slights they receive, real or imagined. And the small slights never stop. They're constant and they need constant forgiveness.

In this holy season, we look at God's immeasurable forgiveness found in the passion and death of Jesus and learn from him. "Father, forgive them for they know not what they do." Seeing God's forgiveness, the saints say, helps us to forgive. He's forgiven us so much. Shouldn't we forgive too?

ST. PAUL OF THE CROSS

"The humility and charity of Father Paul was shown in the way he looked on those who persecuted him over time and tried to discredit him or take away his reputation. In speaking about them or telling a story they had a part in, he remembered what they had done as a kindness. He was grateful for them, in the light of faith, and prayed for them because of the abundant graces they had brought him." (The Life of Blessed Paul of the Cross, by St. Vincent Strambi, chapter 32)

PRAYER

How many times must I forgive today, Lord,
how many times must I be patient, kind, understanding,
willing to carry on even if no one sees or cares?
Bless me with the graces of your passion and death,
especially the grace of forgiveness.
Amen.

GOSPEL

JESUS SAID TO HIS DISCIPLES:

"Do not think that I have come to abolish the law or the prophets. I have come not to abolish but to fulfill. Amen, I say to you, until heaven and earth pass away, not the smallest letter or the smallest part of a letter will pass from the law, until all things have taken place. Therefore, whoever breaks one of the least of these commandments and teaches others to do so will be called least in the Kingdom of heaven. But whoever obeys and teaches these commandments will be called greatest in the Kingdom of heaven."

MATTHEW 5: 17-19

REFLECTION

Jesus ascends a mountain and gathers his disciples to teach them, according to Matthew's Gospel, chapters 5–7. Moses before him brought God's word to the Israelites from a high mountain. Now, Jesus teaches as the New Moses. He does not abolish what the great patriarch taught; he brings it to fulfillment.

Lent gathers us again to listen to the Sermon on the Mount. Sublime promises of a Kingdom are made; our God is gracious and near. But this part of the Gospel reminds us of little things, the small steps, the "least commandments" we must keep to enter the Kingdom of heaven.

This is a season—our reading reminds us—for remembering that small things like a cup of cold water, a visit to the sick, feeding someone hungry, clothing someone naked, speaking a "word to the weary to rouse them" are important commandments of God.

Yes, Lent calls us to think great thoughts and embrace great visions of faith. But the law of God often comes down to small things, and the greatest in the kingdom of God are the best at that.

ST. PAUL OF THE CROSS

"The most important things for you are: humility of heart, patience, meekness, charity toward all, and seeing in your neighbor an image of God and loving him in God and for God" (Letter 1114, March 1, 1758).

PRAYER

What small step do you want me to take today, O Lord?
Let me be small myself, humble of heart and mind
that I can see another's need, not my own.
What can I do to help the neighbor I meet,
my neighbor made in your image?
Amen.

GOSPEL

Jesus was driving out a demon that was mute, and when the demon had gone out, the mute man spoke and the crowds were amazed. Some of them said, "By the power of Beelzebul, the prince of demons, he drives out demons." Others, to test him, asked him for a sign from heaven. But he knew their thoughts and said to them, "Every kingdom divided against itself will be laid waste and house will fall against house. And if Satan is divided against himself, how will his kingdom stand? For you say that it is by Beelzebul that I drive out demons. If I, then, drive out demons by Beelzebul, by whom do your own people drive them out? Therefore they will be your judges. But if it is by the finger of God that I drive out demons, then the Kingdom of God has come upon you. When a strong man fully armed guards his palace, his possessions are safe. But when one stronger than he attacks and overcomes him, he takes away the armor on which he relied and distributes the spoils. Whoever is not with me is against me, and whoever does not gather with me scatters."

LUKE 11: 14-23

REFLECTION

Talk of devils and demons and miracles by God, so common in the bible, sounds strange to people today, especially in the western world. We think other forces are at work when something remarkable happens, as it did to the man who couldn't speak. Must be a natural explanation—maybe the power of suggestion; whatever it was, we'll discover it. We find it hard to see "the finger of God" causing miracles today.

Miracles of healing were among the signs that pointed out Jesus to his early hearers, but they weren't the most important one. After Pentecost, Peter describes Jesus of Nazareth as "a man attested to you by God with deeds of power, wonder and signs that God did through him among you, as you yourselves know," but the culmination of signs, the apostle says, is his own death and Resurrection.

No one can explain this mystery, surpassing all others. Taking on himself all human sorrows—the sorrow of the mute, the deaf, the paralyzed, the possessed, the dead, the sinner far from God—Jesus gave himself into the hands of his heavenly Father on the altar of the cross. And he was raised up and gave his life-giving Spirit to the world.

Some deny this sign too, but it's the great sign that we celebrate in this holy season.

ST. PAUL OF THE CROSS

"Regarding the mysteries of the Passion of our Lord, I advise you to stay with those in which you find more devotion and cause you to love God. But when your soul is pleased to remain in the sacred silence of faith and holy love, resting on the bosom of the Father, follow that inclination, even though it lasts for all your prayer. Obey the Holy Spirit, who draws you in prayer."). (Letter 1188, March 29, 1759)

PRAYER

Where can I see signs of your love and your work, O God?
I have only to begin with myself,
"wondrously, fearfully made,"
from my mother's womb.
Then, there is the Sign of your Son's death and Resurrection,
wondrous and fearful.
Keep it before my eyes, O Lord,
as a promise of life still to come.
Amen.

GOSPEL

One of the scribes came to Jesus and asked him, "Which is the first of all the commandments?" Jesus replied, "The first is this: *Hear, O Israel! The Lord our God is Lord alone! You shall love the Lord your God with all your heart, with all your soul, with all your mind, and with all your strength.* The second is this: *You shall love your neighbor as yourself.* There is no other commandment greater than these." The scribe said to him, "Well said, teacher. You are right in saying, *He is One and there is no other than he.* And *to love him with all your heart, with all your understanding, with all your strength, and to love your neighbor as yourself* is worth more than all burnt offerings and sacrifices." And when Jesus saw that he answered with understanding, he said to him, "You are not far from the Kingdom of God." And no one dared to ask him any more questions.

MARK 12: 28-34

REFLECTION

Love God and love your neighbor, Jesus says in today's Gospel. We would expect to hear about love on a Lenten Friday since every Friday of the year recalls the Friday called Good. The Lenten Fridays especially prepare us for that great day of love.

The Gospels dwell on what took place that day in great detail. Historians, scholars, artists approach the mystery of Jesus' passion and death in different ways. What political or religious factors were behind it? Who were the people involved? The day is a fascinating conclusion to a fascinating life. But, above all, it's a day about love.

Why did Jesus suffer such a death, we ask? As God's Son, no one could take his life from him. The only answer we can give is that Jesus gave himself up to death and he accepted death on the Cross out of love for his Father and out of love for us. Love caused him to say in the Garden, "Your will be done." Love called words of forgiveness from the cross: "Father, forgive them, for they know not what they do."

The cross was not something Jesus endured; he embraced it with his whole heart, his whole mind and all his strength. At his cross, we stand before Love. With love we should approach the cross, says St. Paul of the Cross.

ST. PAUL OF THE CROSS

"When you experience dryness in your prayer, gently stir your spirit with loving acts then rest in God. Softly say to him, 'How bruised your face, how swollen, how disfigured with spit. I see your bones laid bare. What suffering, what blows, what grief. Love is one great wound. Sweet are your wounds, sweet is your suffering. I want to keep you always close to my heart'" (Letter 23, March 17, 1734).

PRAYER

Lord Jesus Christ,
I love you, who loved me and all the world.
Amen.

GOSPEL

Jesus addressed this parable to those who were convinced of their own righteousness and despised everyone else. "Two people went up to the temple area to pray; one was a Pharisee and the other was a tax collector. The Pharisee took up his position and spoke this prayer to himself, 'O God, I thank you that I am not like the rest of humanity—greedy, dishonest, adulterous—or even like this tax collector. I fast twice a week, and I pay tithes on my whole income.' But the tax collector stood off at a distance and would not even raise his eyes to heaven but beat his breast and prayed, 'O God, be merciful to me a sinner.' I tell you, the latter went home justified, not the former; for everyone who exalts himself will be humbled, and the one who humbles himself will be exalted."

LUKE 18: 9-14

REFLECTION

Luke's Gospel presents Jesus as often siding with those who are so let down by life and their own faults that they hardly dream of anything better—tax collectors, widows, sinners like the prodigal son. They were beaten down souls. He was criticized frequently by others for associating with people like that, so he must have done it often enough.

The tax collector in the parable, praying in the back of the temple is an example. Luke recalls earlier in his Gospel that Jesus sat down at table with Matthew and some of his tax collector friends in Capernaum. Was Jesus telling their story in this parable?

Staying at a distance, eyes down, the tax collector says only a few words: "O God, be merciful to me a sinner."

The Pharisee's prayer is so different, so full of himself; he seems to ask only for applause and approval. The tax collector asks only for mercy.

His prayer is heard so shouldn't we make it our own? Tax-collectors, widows and sinners stand closest to where all humanity stands. We all need God's mercy. We come to God empty-handed.

"O God come to my assistance. O Lord make haste to help me."

St. Paul of the Cross saw the tax collector kneeling humbly before God as someone we should kneel beside.

ST. PAUL OF THE CROSS

"I wish that you remain in your horrible nothingness, knowing that you have nothing, can do nothing and know nothing. God doesn't do anything for those who wish to be something; but one who is aware of his nothingness in truth, is ready. 'If anyone thinks himself to be something, he deceives himself,' said the Apostle, whose name I bear unworthily" (Letter 1033, July 20, 1756).

PRAYER

"O God, be merciful to me, a sinner."
Amen.

FOURTH WEEK
OF
LENT

GOSPEL

As Jesus passed by he saw a man blind from birth. His disciples asked him, "Rabbi, who sinned, this man or his parents, that he was born blind?" Jesus answered, "Neither he nor his parents sinned; it is so that the works of God might be made visible through him. We have to do the works of the one who sent me while it is day. Night is coming when no one can work. While I am in the world, I am the light of the world." When he had said this, he spat on the ground and made clay with the saliva, and smeared the clay on his eyes, and said to him, "Go wash in the Pool of Siloam" —which means Sent.— So he went and washed, and came back able to see.

His neighbors and those who had seen him earlier as a beggar said, "Isn't this the one who used to sit and beg?" Some said, "It is," but others said, "No, he just looks like him." He said, "I am." So they said to him, "How were your eyes opened?" He replied, "The man called Jesus made clay and anointed my eyes and told me, 'Go to Siloam and wash.' So I went there and washed and was able to see." And they said to him, "Where is he?" He said, "I don't know."

They brought the one who was once blind to the Pharisees. Now Jesus had made clay and opened his eyes on a sabbath. So then the Pharisees also asked him how he was able to see. He said to them, "He put clay on my eyes, and I washed, and now I can see." So some of the Pharisees said, "This man is not from God, because he does not keep the sabbath." But others said, "How can a sinful man do such signs?" And there was a division among them. So they said to the blind man again, "What do you have to say about him, since he opened your eyes?" He said, "He is a prophet."

Now the Jews did not believe that he had been blind and gained his sight until they summoned the parents of the one who had gained his sight. They asked them, "Is this your son, who you say was born blind? How does he now see?" His parents answered and said, "We know that this is our son and that he was born blind. We do not know how he sees now, nor do we know who opened his eyes. Ask him, he is of age; he can speak for himself." His parents said this because they were afraid of the Jews, for the Jews had already agreed that if anyone acknowledged him as the Christ, he would be expelled from the synagogue. For this reason his parents said, "He is of age; question him."

So a second time they called the man who had been blind and said to him, "Give God the praise! We know that this man is a sinner." He replied, "If he is a sinner, I do not know. One thing I do know is that I was blind and now I see." So they said to him, "What did he do to you? How did he open your eyes?" He answered them, "I told you already and you did not listen. Why do you want to hear it again? Do you want to become his disciples, too?" They ridiculed him and said, "You are that man's disciple; we are disciples of Moses! We know that God spoke to Moses, but we do not know where this one is from." The man answered and said to them, "This is what is so amazing, that you do not know where he is from, yet he opened my eyes. We know that God does not listen to sinners, but if one is devout and does his will, he listens to him. It is unheard of that anyone ever opened the eyes of a person born blind. If this man were not from God, he would not be able to do anything." They answered and said to him, "You were born totally in sin, and are you trying to teach us?" Then they threw him out.

When Jesus heard that they had thrown him out, he found him and said, "Do you believe in the Son of Man?" He answered and said, "Who is he, sir, that I may believe in him?" Jesus said to him, "You have seen him, the one speaking with you is he." He said, "I do believe, Lord," and he worshiped him. Then Jesus said, "I came into this world for judgment, so that those who do not see might see, and those who do see might become blind."

Some of the Pharisees who were with him heard this and said to him, "Surely we are not also blind, are we?" Jesus said to them, "If you were blind, you would have no sin; but now you are saying, 'We see,' so your sin remains."

JOHN 9: 1-41

Shorter form: JOHN 9:1, 6-9, 13-17, 34-38
Longer form may be optionally read on any day in the fourth week of Lent

REFLECTION

This is a dramatic Gospel, not only because of the miracle, but because of the heated exchanges and clever dialogue found in it. Jesus and his disciples, the blind man himself, his parents and neighbors and a divided group of Pharisees all interact vigorously in the story.

Unlike others, this blind man did not approach Jesus. Rather, Jesus approached him. And remarkably, the miracle did not just restore the man's sight. Blind from birth, he never before had the power to see. Could he represent those who can do nothing for themselves? Nothing at all, except wait for the power of God? He could be all of us.

At the sight of the woebegone beggar, Jesus' disciples wondered: did he do something to deserve it? Some sin he or his parents had committed? No, Jesus replied. "He was born blind so that God's power might be displayed in curing him."

It was Jesus' message always: God wills to display his power in the poor. God's power—healing, restoring, creating—goes out to the blind man and others like him. And as Jesus dispensed this power, so too he told his disciples "to carry on while daylight lasts the work of him who sent me."

It's God's power, not ours, that's given to the poor. As Jesus' disciples, we must work to share it with others. Then, perhaps, some of its blessing will fall on us. After all, none of us is far from the poor blind beggar.

ST. PAUL OF THE CROSS

"Humbly see your nothingness, never lose sight of it. Then, when His Divine Majesty makes it disappear in the Infinite All that is himself, stay there lost without seeing who you are any more. It's not important. Follow his divine inspirations. The less you understand, the more ignorant you are in this school, the more learned you become. Neither you or any creature can know the grandeur of God and the divine impression he makes on humble hearts because he delights in them" (Letter 929, December 21, 1754).

PRAYER

Lord,
I am blind;
Help me to see.
Amen.

GOSPEL

JESUS SAID TO NICODEMUS:

"Just as Moses lifted up the serpent in the desert, so must the Son of Man be lifted up, so that everyone who believes in him may have eternal life."

For God so loved the world that he gave his only Son, so that everyone who believes in him might not perish but might have eternal life. For God did not send his Son into the world to condemn the world, but that the world might be saved through him. Whoever believes in him will not be condemned, but whoever does not believe has already been condemned, because he has not believed in the name of the only Son of God. And this is the verdict, that the light came into the world, but people preferred darkness to light, because their works were evil. For everyone who does wicked things hates the light and does not come toward the light, so that his works might not be exposed. But whoever lives the truth comes to the light, so that his works may be clearly seen as done in God.

JOHN 3: 14-21

REFLECTION

Like Nicodemus, we are often in the dark about God and his ways with us. That's why we listen carefully to the words of today's Gospel: "God so loved the world that he gave his only Son."

Who are we? Insignificant creatures who, like spring flowers, pass quickly away. We're sinners who misuse the gracious gifts that we've been given. History paints a sad picture of our failures. Why should God love us?

Who is God? The One who dwells in light inaccessible, infinitely wise and powerful. Why should he love us who are so small? Even more, why should he send his only Son, equal to him in all things, to save us?

God's love appears when Jesus is lifted up on a cross, an unlikely sign of love. John's Gospel takes a similar unlikely sign from the Old Testament to express it. On their journey through the desert, the Jews murmur against God about the manna he sends them, and they're bitten by snakes that bring them death. They repent, and Moses is told to put a serpent on a staff; whoever looks on it lives. An image of death brings life.

In our lives too, God's love comes in the good things he sends, but also in the crosses of suffering and disappointment we must bear. Through these signs of death God bring us life. St. Paul of the Cross recommends that we see our crosses as life-giving.

ST. PAUL OF THE CROSS

"That soul is very fortunate who feeds in spirit and truth on the divine Manna of God's will, accepting all that happens as God's will fulfilled, no matter how bitter it is. When you see things with the eye of faith, the greatest bitterness, the storms that afflict soul and body, become joys gushing from the side of holy Love" (Letter 920, September 3, 1754).

PRAYER

Lord Jesus,
the mystery of your Cross
promises that sorrow will be turned into joy.
Take the sorrows of our world
and place them in your holy wounds
and loving heart.
Bring them life through your death.
Amen.

GOSPEL

Tax collectors and sinners were all drawing near to listen to Jesus, but the Pharisees and scribes began to complain, saying, "This man welcomes sinners and eats with them." So to them Jesus addressed this parable: "A man had two sons, and the younger son said to his father, 'Father, give me the share of your estate that should come to me.' So the father divided the property between them. After a few days, the younger son collected all his belongings and set off to a distant country where he squandered his inheritance on a life of dissipation. When he had freely spent everything, a severe famine struck that country, and he found himself in dire need. So he hired himself out to one of the local citizens who sent him to his farm to tend the swine. And he longed to eat his fill of the pods on which the swine fed, but nobody gave him any. Coming to his senses he thought, 'How many of my father's hired workers have more than enough food to eat, but here am I, dying from hunger. I shall get up and go to my father and I shall say to him, "Father, I have sinned against heaven and against you. I no longer deserve to be called your son; treat me as you would treat one of your hired workers."' So he got up and went back to his father. While he was still a long way off, his father caught sight of him, and was filled with compassion. He ran to his son, embraced him and kissed him. His son said to him, 'Father, I have sinned against heaven and against you; I no longer deserve to be called your son.' But his father ordered his servants, 'Quickly, bring the finest robe and put it on him; put a ring on his finger and sandals on his feet. Take the fattened calf and slaughter it. Then let us celebrate with a feast, because this son of mine was dead, and has come to life again; he was lost, and has been found.' Then the celebration began. Now the older son had been out in the field and, on his way back, as he neared the house, he heard the sound of music and dancing. He called one of the servants and asked what this might mean. The servant said to him, 'Your brother has returned and your father has slaughtered the fattened calf because he has him back safe and sound.' He became angry, and when he refused to enter the house, his father came out and pleaded with him. He said to his father in reply, 'Look, all these years I served you and not once did I disobey your orders; yet you never gave me even a young goat to feast on with my friends. But when your son returns who swallowed up your property with prostitutes, for him you slaughter the fattened calf.' He said to him, 'My son, you are here with me always; everything I have is yours. But now we must celebrate and rejoice, because your brother was dead and has come to life again; he was lost and has been found.'"

LUKE 15: 1-3, 11-32

REFLECTION

We have to hear certain stories over and over. One of them is the story of the prodigal son. Actually, it could also be called the story of the prodigal father.

The word "prodigal" can be taken in two ways. It can mean someone who's wasteful, extravagant, and improvident; words we can rightly apply to the son who leaves his father's house. Or prodigal can also mean someone who is generous, unstinting, and unsparing.

The father is prodigal in that second sense of the word. He's generous with the freedom he gives his son in allowing him to leave home so well provided for. He's unstinting in his patience as we waits for his son's return. He's unsparing in the welcome he gives him when he comes back home.

"Quickly bring the finest robe and put it on him; put a ring on his finger and sandals on his feet. Kill the fattened calf and slaughter it. Then let us celebrate, because this son of mine was dead and has come back to life; he was lost and has been found."

No threats, no punishment, no recriminations, no disowning of the wayward boy. He's still his father's son shining in his new robes, a ring on his finger that's proof he belongs, sandals on his feet that give him freedom to walk again.

God is like that. His mercy is beyond what we imagine. We have to hear about it over and over. St. Paul of the Cross saw preaching as a proclamation of God's mercy.

ST. PAUL OF THE CROSS

"It's not difficult to see what effect the preaching of Father Paul and his brother had; the sight of them alone was a sermon. The two missionaries came from their solitude in rough garments; their uncovered heads and bare feet recalled John the Baptist who preached a gospel of peace. Their toils were unceasing; wherever they preached crowds followed them, asking them to hear their confessions and reconcile them to God.

Their hardest labors were along the coast of Tuscany, which teemed with bandits and robbers. Seeing the miserable state of these unhappy men, Father Paul devoted his days and nights to helping them and he treated them with marvelous kindness and gentleness. (Life of Blessed Paul of the Cross, by St. Vincent Strambi, Chapter 11)

PRAYER

God, our Father,
like the son who got lost in a distant land
I stray away from you.
Give me the grace to return to you
and help me to believe in your mercy.
Amen.

Gospel

At that time Jesus left [Samaria] for Galilee. For Jesus himself testified that a prophet has no honor in his native place. When he came into Galilee, the Galileans welcomed him, since they had seen all he had done in Jerusalem at the feast; for they themselves had gone to the feast.

Then he returned to Cana in Galilee, where he had made the water wine. Now there was a royal official whose son was ill in Capernaum. When he heard that Jesus had arrived in Galilee from Judea, he went to him and asked him to come down and heal his son, who was near death. Jesus said to him, "Unless you people see signs and wonders, you will not believe." The royal official said to him, "Sir, come down before my child dies." Jesus said to him, "You may go; your son will live." The man believed what Jesus said to him and left. While the man was on his way back, his slaves met him and told him that his boy would live. He asked them when he began to recover. They told him, "The fever left him yesterday, about one in the afternoon." The father realized that just at that time Jesus had said to him, "Your son will live," and he and his whole household came to believe. Now this was the second sign Jesus did when he came to Galilee from Judea.

John 4: 43-54

REFLECTION

The Church in its Good Friday liturgy tells the story of the passion and death of Jesus from the Gospel of John, and the same Gospel is also read on the days leading up to this great mystery, beginning on Monday of the fourth week of Lent and continuing into Holy Week.

John's readings cast a subtle light on the final story of the Word made flesh. Today's reading about the government official who begs Jesus to come and heal his son is not an isolated incident separated from everything else. It's a sign related to the miracle in Cana in Galilee, where the water was changed into wine. It's also a sign—the second sign from Cana—related to Jesus' death and Resurrection.

"Your son will live," Jesus tells the government official. The father seeking life for his son is an image of the Father whose love will not let death claim his Son but brings him to life again. In John's Gospel, Jesus affirms repeatedly his union with his Father. "The Father and I are one." "My Father is at work until now, so I am at work." It's a theme we'll hear often in these final days of Lent.

God is not heartless before the mystery of death. Can our Father in heaven be less loving than the father at Cana in Galilee pleading for the life of his son? God infinitely surpasses the powerful government official. The Father of Jesus, our Father, never wavers; he brings us life.

John's Gospel was a favorite source for St. Paul of the Cross who sees our spiritual journey in the light of Jesus' journey to his death and Resurrection. We have another life before us, so we must mystically die to this one. We're called to rest in the bosom of the Father.

ST. PAUL OF THE CROSS

"I recommend to you never to rest in the gifts or the joy of spirit such gifts of God bring, but with one sweet glance of faith and love journey further to God in nakedness and poverty of spirit, losing all in him, not looking back on your suffering or on any spiritual understanding you have, but rest in naked faith and pure love on the bosom of God, completely clothed in Jesus Crucified" (Letter 914, July 23, 1754).

PRAYER

O God,
we cannot rest until we rest in you,
so give me a restless heart,
for the journey I'm on.
Free me from what holds me,
what slows my steps.
Give me faith to seek and find you,
following your only Son.
Amen.

GOSPEL

There was a feast of the Jews, and Jesus went up to Jerusalem. Now there is in Jerusalem at the Sheep Gate a pool called in Hebrew Bethesda, with five porticoes. In these lay a large number of ill, blind, lame, and crippled. One man was there who had been ill for thirty-eight years. When Jesus saw him lying there and knew that he had been ill for a long time, he said to him, "Do you want to be well?" The sick man answered him, "Sir, I have no one to put me into the pool when the water is stirred up; while I am on my way, someone else gets down there before me." Jesus said to him, "Rise, take up your mat, and walk." Immediately the man became well, took up his mat, and walked.

Now that day was a sabbath. So the Jews said to the man who was cured, "It is the sabbath, and it is not lawful for you to carry your mat." He answered them, "The man who made me well told me, 'Take up your mat and walk.'" They asked him, "Who is the man who told you, 'Take it up and walk'?" The man who was healed did not know who it was, for Jesus had slipped away, since there was a crowd there. After this Jesus found him in the temple area and said to him, "Look, you are well; do not sin any more, so that nothing worse may happen to you." The man went and told the Jews that Jesus was the one who had made him well. Therefore, the Jews began to persecute Jesus because he did this on a sabbath.

JOHN 5: 1-16

REFLECTION

Let's compare the paralyzed man at the pool at Bethesda with the official in our previous story from John's Gospel, who came from Capernaum to Cana in Galilee seeking a cure for his son. Obviously, the official was important. He knew how to get things done and came to get Jesus to do something for him. He's a resourceful man.

The paralytic at Bethesda, on the other hand, seems utterly resourceless. For thirty-eight years he's come to a healing pool— archeologists identify its location near the present church of St. Anne in Jerusalem— and he can't find a way into the water when it's stirring. Paralyzed, too slow, he can't even get anybody to help him. He doesn't approach Jesus; Jesus approaches him, asking: "Do you want to be well?"

Instead of lowering him into the water, Jesus cures the paralyzed man directly and tells him to take up the mat he was lying on and walk. The man has no idea who cured him until Jesus tells him later in the temple area. He's slow in more ways than one.

"God chose what is weak in the world to shame the strong; God chose what is low and despised in this world, things that are not, to reduce to nothing things that are, so that no one might boast in the presence of God," St. Paul tells the Corinthians.

Here's one of the weak, the lowly, the nobodies God chooses, and he won't be the only one.

The mystics saw weakness differently than most do. It was a time for God to act, as St. Paul of the Cross once wrote:

ST. PAUL OF THE CROSS

"Be of good heart, my good friend, for the time has come for you to be cured. Night will be as illumined as day. As his night, so is his day. A great difference takes place in the Presence of God; rejoice in this Divine Presence. Have nothing, my dear one; allow yourself to be deprived of all pleasure. Do not look your sufferings in the face, but accept them with resignation and satisfaction in the higher part of your soul as if they were jewels, and so they truly are. Ah! let your loving soul be freed from all that is created and pay no attention to suffering or to enjoyment, but give your attention to your beloved Good" (Letter 41, September 7, 1729).

PRAYER

Lord Jesus,
like the paralytic I wait for you,
not knowing when or how you will come,
unable to help myself.
But I wait, O Lord,
however long you may be.
Amen.

GOSPEL

Jesus answered the Jews: "My Father is at work until now, so I am at work." For this reason they tried all the more to kill him, because he not only broke the sabbath but he also called God his own father, making himself equal to God.

Jesus answered and said to them, "Amen, amen, I say to you, the Son cannot do anything on his own, but only what he sees the Father doing; for what he does, the Son will do also. For the Father loves the Son and shows him everything that he himself does, and he will show him greater works than these, so that you may be amazed. For just as the Father raises the dead and gives life, so also does the Son give life to whomever he wishes. Nor does the Father judge anyone, but he has given all judgment to the Son, so that all may honor the Son just as they honor the Father. Whoever does not honor the Son does not honor the Father who sent him. Amen, amen, I say to you, whoever hears my word and believes in the one who sent me has eternal life and will not come to condemnation, but has passed from death to life. Amen, amen, I say to you, the hour is coming and is now here when the dead will hear the voice of the Son of God, and those who hear will live. For just as the Father has life in himself, so also he gave to the Son the possession of life in himself. And he gave him power to exercise judgment, because he is the Son of Man. Do not be amazed at this, because the hour is coming in which all who are in the tombs will hear his voice and will come out, those who have done good deeds to the resurrection of life, but those who have done wicked deeds to the resurrection of condemnation.

"I cannot do anything on my own; I judge as I hear, and my judgment is just, because I do not seek my own will but the will of the one who sent me."

JOHN 5: 17-30

REFLECTION

The cure of the paralyzed man at the pool of Bethsaida set off criticism of Jesus by the Jewish leaders in Jerusalem who accuse him of working on the Sabbath. Already, rabbis had questioned an absolute proscription of Sabbath work; after all, God maintained creation on the Sabbath, babies were born, people died, God's judgment went on for that day.

But the leaders' criticism was based on a greater charge—Jesus claimed to be God's Son. He said he continued his Father's work; he had power over life and death; he will judge the living and the dead. These are divine powers.

"Who do you say I am?" is a question Jesus asked then and he asks us now. John's Gospel will give answers to that question in the readings that follow for the remainder of this week and into Holy Week.

"Who do you say I am?" is an important question we ask when we look at the One who dies on the cross. In our public prayers we say:

He is the Word of God, through whom you made the universe,
the Savior you sent to redeem us . . .
For our sake he opened his arms on the cross,
He put an end to death,
And revealed the Resurrection (Eucharistic Prayer 2).

Our personal prayer too rests on this powerful belief, as we see in the writings of Paul of the Cross.

ST. PAUL OF THE CROSS

"Often turn to our holy faith and let it lead you into the bosom and the arms of God. You'll be blessed if you faithfully follow my advice. When affliction lays heavy on you, you can go to your room, take the crucifix in your hands and give yourself a sermon from it. What a sermon you will hear! How quickly your heart will be calmed" (Letter 1464, May 26, 1764).

PRAYER

Lord Jesus,
I come before your Cross
asking who you are.
You are God's Son,
true God from true God,
maker of all, and beyond us all.
Yet, here you are
One like us,
dying on a cross.
My Lord and my God!
Amen.

GOSPEL

JESUS SAID TO THE JEWS:

"If I testify on my own behalf, my testimony is not true. But there is another who testifies on my behalf, and I know that the testimony he gives on my behalf is true. You sent emissaries to John, and he testified to the truth. I do not accept human testimony, but I say this so that you may be saved. He was a burning and shining lamp, and for a while you were content to rejoice in his light. But I have testimony greater than John's. The works that the Father gave me to accomplish, these works that I perform testify on my behalf that the Father has sent me. Moreover, the Father who sent me has testified on my behalf. But you have never heard his voice nor seen his form, and you do not have his word remaining in you, because you do not believe in the one whom he has sent. You search the Scriptures, because you think you have eternal life through them; even they testify on my behalf. But you do not want to come to me to have life.

"I do not accept human praise; moreover, I know that you do not have the love of God in you. I came in the name of my Father, but you do not accept me; yet if another comes in his own name, you will accept him. How can you believe, when you accept praise from one another and do not seek the praise that comes from the only God? Do not think that I will accuse you before the Father: the one who will accuse you is Moses, in whom you have placed your hope. For if you had believed Moses, you would have believed me, because he wrote about me. But if you do not believe his writings, how will you believe my words?"

JOHN 5: 31-47

REFLECTION

Different witnesses take the stand in today's Gospel testifying for Jesus and we listen to them. John the Baptist, "a burning and shining lamp," speaks for him. The miracles and works of healing Jesus performed testify for him. Above all, his heavenly Father, who draws to his Son those unhindered by pride, through an interior call, speaks for him. Then, the scriptures, long searched by the Jews as the way to eternal life, "testify on my behalf."

These are ways faith in Jesus comes to us now. Do we accept them? The church, like John the Baptist, points Jesus Christ out to us; are we guided by its light? His works and words and miracles are proclaimed in the scriptures; do we search into them? Our heavenly Father draws us to his Son; do we pray for faith and humility to accept his grace?

We're reminded by scholars that "the Jews" spoken of in these passages of John's Gospel are not the whole Jewish nation but those who opposed Jesus because pride and position turned them against him. Ever since, people still oppose him. In Lent, the voice of the Father says once more: "Listen to him."

Mystics like Paul of the Cross knew that faith is a gift of God; we don't get it by reason alone. He recommended prayer, steady prayer, as a means to gain, to nourish and strengthen faith.

ST. PAUL OF THE CROSS

"Someone who left his community once wrote to Fr. Paul and signed the letter pretentiously, Archpriest, Lawyer, Theologian. Answering his letter, Fr. Paul signed himself, N.N.N., which means Paul of the Cross, who is nothing, who knows nothing, can do nothing, desires nothing in this world but Jesus Christ, and him crucified. This was his wisdom: to see with eyes of faith his own nothingness and to allow God who works within us to be born there." (Life of Blessed Paul of the Cross, by St. Vincent Strambi, Chapter 35)

PRAYER

O God,
I come to you
who have given so much to me.
You know "my inmost being"
and "all my thoughts from afar."
I want to listen to you
and be changed by what I hear.
Amen.

GOSPEL

Jesus moved about within Galilee; he did not wish to travel in Judea, because the Jews were trying to kill him. But the Jewish feast of Tabernacles was near.

But when his brothers had gone up to the feast, he himself also went up, not openly but as it were in secret.

Some of the inhabitants of Jerusalem said, "Is he not the one they are trying to kill? And look, he is speaking openly and they say nothing to him. Could the authorities have realized that he is the Christ? But we know where he is from. When the Christ comes, no one will know where he is from." So Jesus cried out in the temple area as he was teaching and said, "You know me and also know where I am from. Yet I did not come on my own, but the one who sent me, whom you do not know, is true. I know him, because I am from him, and he sent me." So they tried to arrest him, but no one laid a hand upon him, because his hour had not yet come.

JOHN 7: 1-2, 10, 25-30

REFLECTION

From Galilee Jesus went up to Jerusalem where "the Jews were trying to kill him" to celebrate the feast of Tabernacles, a popular autumn feast drawing crowds of visitors to the city. He immediately draws the attention of "the inhabitants of the city." Who are they?

They're not the leaders who will later put him to death. They're the ordinary public who watch the leaders, who know what's happening in the city, who follow the trends and pass the gossip. They watch Jesus with curiosity as he enters the temple area and begins to teach.

"Do our leaders now believe he's the Messiah?" "How can he be, because he's from Galilee and no one will know where the Messiah is from?" Here are the voices of those who go back and forth, the undecided who wait to see who wins before taking sides.

Jesus cried out against them, because they think they know what's going on but know nothing. They're blind to the Word in their midst.

Prayer helps us to see what is real, the spiritual masters teach, but to see what is real we must first put aside the ordinary ways we see and judge and act. Unfortunately, ordinary thinking often blinds us to the truth. Whether we're learned theologians, practiced priests, informed church-goers, or "inhabitants of Jerusalem" we need to humble ourselves before God. Prayer is a way of taking sides, the right side.

ST. PAUL OF THE CROSS

"Let us remain in our nothingness; we have nothing, we're able to do nothing, we know nothing. Then, God will draw from this nothingness works to his greater glory" (Letter 1033, July 20, 1756).

PRAYER

Lord, have mercy.
Christ, have mercy.
Lord, have mercy.

My words, Lord,
words of one "who has nothing,
is able do nothing, knows nothing."
In your mercy, hear me.
Amen.

GOSPEL

Some in the crowd who heard these words of Jesus said, "This is truly the Prophet." Others said, "This is the Christ." But others said, "The Christ will not come from Galilee, will he? Does not Scripture say that the Christ will be of David's family and come from Bethlehem, the village where David lived?" So a division occurred in the crowd because of him. Some of them even wanted to arrest him, but no one laid hands on him.

So the guards went to the chief priests and Pharisees, who asked them, "Why did you not bring him?" The guards answered, "Never before has anyone spoken like this man." So the Pharisees answered them, "Have you also been deceived? Have any of the authorities or the Pharisees believed in him? But this crowd, which does not know the law, is accursed." Nicodemus, one of their members who had come to him earlier, said to them, "Does our law condemn a man before it first hears him and finds out what he is doing?" They answered and said to him, "You are not from Galilee also, are you? Look and see that no prophet arises from Galilee."

Then each went to his own house.

JOHN 7: 40-53

REFLECTION

The readings from John's Gospel for today and through the next week of Lent (chapters 7–10) sum up Jesus' activity in Jerusalem during the eight-day Feast of Tabernacles, the popular autumn feast that brought many visitors to the city to celebrate the grape harvest and pray for rain. Water was brought into the temple courtyard from the Pool of Siloam and lighted torches were ablaze during the celebration.

Arriving a few days late, Jesus taught in the temple area and revealed who he was, using the themes of water and light. His cure of the blind man, in the ninth chapter of the Gospel, is a sign of the light he bestows on a blind world.

Yet, some do not see. His message and miracles divide his hearers; some want him arrested, some believe, some question his Galilean origins and his upbringing as a carpenter's son. How can he be the Messiah, a teacher in Israel?

We're surprised at the unbelief before the glory that surrounds the Word of God on his way from Nazareth to Jerusalem. Why didn't all see it and believe? People doubted him then, our reading reminds us, and they will doubt him now. Even his disciples are slow to believe. "How slow you are to believe." Jesus says to two of them on the way to Emmaus.

But the Word continues to teach in our world and to instruct disciples weak in faith. His mission does not end. Saints like Paul of the Cross knew that. However fierce the opposition, the Word of God, Jesus Christ, brings light and life.

ST. PAUL OF THE CROSS

"All the works of God are now attacked by the devil, now by human beings. I now have both at once. Don't be dismayed when contrary factions and rejections arise, no matter how great they are. Be encouraged by the example of St. Teresa who said that the more she was involved in enterprises for the glory of God, the more difficulties she experienced" (Letter 1180, February 1, 1759).

PRAYER

The Lord is my light and my salvation,
Whom should I fear?
The Lord is the stronghold of my life,
Of whom should I be afraid?
Amen.

FIFTH WEEK
OF
LENT

GOSPEL

Now a man was ill, Lazarus from Bethany, the village of Mary and her sister Martha. Mary was the one who had anointed the Lord with perfumed oil and dried his feet with her hair; it was her brother Lazarus who was ill. So the sisters sent word to Jesus saying, "Master, the one you love is ill." When Jesus heard this he said, "This illness is not to end in death, but is for the glory of God, that the Son of God may be glorified through it." Now Jesus loved Martha and her sister and Lazarus. So when he heard that he was ill, he remained for two days in the place where he was. Then after this he said to his disciples, "Let us go back to Judea." The disciples said to him, "Rabbi, the Jews were just trying to stone you, and you want to go back there?" Jesus answered, "Are there not twelve hours in a day? If one walks during the day, he does not stumble, because he sees the light of this world. But if one walks at night, he stumbles, because the light is not in him." He said this, and then told them, "Our friend Lazarus is asleep, but I am going to awaken him." So the disciples said to him, "Master, if he is asleep, he will be saved." But Jesus was talking about his death, while they thought that he meant ordinary sleep. So then Jesus said to them clearly, "Lazarus has died. And I am glad for you that I was not there, that you may believe. Let us go to him." So Thomas, called Didymus, said to his fellow disciples, "Let us also go to die with him."

When Jesus arrived, he found that Lazarus had already been in the tomb for four days. Now Bethany was near Jerusalem, only about two miles away. And many of the Jews had come to Martha and Mary to comfort them about their brother. When Martha heard that Jesus was coming, she went to meet him; but Mary sat at home. Martha said to Jesus, "Lord, if you had been here, my brother would not have died. But even now I know that whatever you ask of God, God will give you."

Jesus said to her, "Your brother will rise." Martha said to him, "I know he will rise, in the resurrection on the last day." Jesus told her, "I am the resurrection and the life; whoever believes in me, even if he dies, will live, and everyone who lives and believes in me will never die. Do you believe this?" She said to him, "Yes, Lord. I have come to believe that you are the Christ, the Son of God, the one who is coming into the world."

When she had said this, she went and called her sister Mary secretly, saying, "The teacher is here and is asking for you." As soon as she heard this, she rose quickly and went to him. For Jesus had not yet come into the village, but was still where Martha had met him. So when the Jews who were with her in the house comforting her saw Mary get up quickly and go out, they followed her, presuming that she was going to the tomb to weep there. When Mary came to where Jesus was and saw him, she fell at his feet and said to him, "Lord, if you had been here, my brother would not have died." When Jesus saw her weeping and the Jews who had come with her weeping, he became perturbed and deeply troubled, and said, "Where have you laid him?" They said to him, "Sir, come and see." And Jesus wept. So the Jews said, "See how he loved him." But some of them said, "Could not the one who opened the eyes of the blind man have done something so that this man would not have died?"

So Jesus, perturbed again, came to the tomb. It was a cave, and a stone lay across it. Jesus said, "Take away the stone." Martha, the dead man's sister, said to him, "Lord, by now there will be a stench; he has been dead for four days." Jesus said to her, "Did I not tell you that if you believe you will see the glory of God?" So they took away the stone. And Jesus raised his eyes and said, "Father, I thank you for hearing me. I know that you always hear me; but because of the crowd here I have said this, that they may believe that you sent me." And when he had said this, he cried out in a loud voice, "Lazarus, come out!" The dead man came out, tied hand and foot with burial bands, and his face was wrapped in a cloth. So Jesus said to them, "Untie him and let him go."

> Now many of the Jews who had come to Mary and seen what he had done began to believe in him.
>
> JOHN 11: 1-45

Shorter form: JOHN 11:3-7, 17, 20-27, 33b-45
Longer form may be optionally read on any day in the fifth week of Lent

REFLECTION

The wonderful story of the death and Resurrection of Lazarus helps us appreciate the mystery of Jesus' death and Resurrection. Lazarus belongs to an influential family that welcomed Jesus to their home in Bethany, a village about two miles from Jerusalem. Martha and Mary were his sisters. Jesus stayed with them when he visited the Holy City.

When Lazarus died some days before the Passover, Jesus had left Jerusalem because of threats to his life and was staying in the safety of the Transjordan, the region where John the Baptist had baptized. Notified of his friend's death, Jesus returned to Bethany, unconcerned for himself.

Death in its many forms was what Jesus came to take away, our Gospel wants us to understand, and the dead Lazarus was a sign of what he wishes to do for all humanity. Lazarus was his friend, but Jesus, the Word made flesh, befriends the whole human race.

In the stirring conclusion of today's Gospel, Jesus calls the dead Lazarus from the tomb and "the dead man came out," bound with the burial cloths that claimed him for death. "Untie him and let him go," Jesus says. Those powerful, hopeful words are said to us too. We are called, not to die, but to live.

Later, on Calvary Jesus himself becomes our sign. A painful death does not claim him, nor will the grave hold him. He is our hope.

The same hope nourished Paul of the Cross.

ST. PAUL OF THE CROSS

"You ask me how I'm doing. I'm more sick than well and full of ailments. I can hardly write this . . . [but] *I find it very good. Bearing the chains, the ropes, the blows, the scourges, the wounds, the thorns, the cross and death of my Savior, I fly to the bosom of the Father, where the gentle Jesus always is, and I allow myself to be lost in his immense Divinity"* (Letter 1925, November 26, 1770).

PRAYER

Like Martha, the sister of Lazarus, O Lord,
I believe you are the Resurrection and the Life.
Amen.

GOSPEL

Some Greeks who had come to worship at the Passover Feast came to Philip, who was from Bethsaida in Galilee, and asked him, "Sir, we would like to see Jesus." Philip went and told Andrew; then Andrew and Philip went and told Jesus. Jesus answered them, "The hour has come for the Son of Man to be glorified. Amen, amen, I say to you, unless a grain of wheat falls to the ground and dies, it remains just a grain of wheat; but if it dies, it produces much fruit. Whoever loves his life loses it, and whoever hates his life in this world will preserve it for eternal life. Whoever serves me must follow me, and where I am, there also will my servant be. The Father will honor whoever serves me.

"I am troubled now. Yet what should I say? 'Father, save me from this hour'? But it was for this purpose that I came to this hour. Father, glorify your name." Then a voice came from heaven, "I have glorified it and will glorify it again." The crowd there heard it and said it was thunder; but others said, "An angel has spoken to him." Jesus answered and said, "This voice did not come for my sake but for yours. Now is the time of judgement on this world; now the ruler of this world will be driven out. And when I am lifted up from the earth, I will draw everyone to myself." He said this indicating the kind of death he would die.

JOHN 12: 20-33

REFLECTION

Our Gospel today is part of the Palm Sunday event, when Jesus enters Jerusalem and crowds acclaim him by casting palm branches before him, crying "Hosanna to the Son of David."

But Jesus is troubled as he enters the city: Jerusalem's leaders mean to kill him. Then, unexpectedly, a sign strengthens him, a simple sign. Some Greeks approach Philip and Andrew and say, "We would like to see Jesus." In their coming, Jesus sees the lasting fruitfulness of his mission on earth. "Like a grain of wheat I will fall to the ground and die."

The Gospel of John is known for signs like this, signs that point to glory. The signs say it is not the end, but the beginning. The Greeks who come as Jesus approaches death are like the Magi at his birth— people from afar, the first of many. Others will come from the east and the west, from countries beyond his own. Some signs in John's Gospel are great miracles, some are small like the visit of the Greeks to Jesus.

Often in his life, Paul of the Cross saw small signs that gave him hope. In a letter to a bishop, the saint recalls what he experienced when Pope Benedict XIV was elected pope in 1740. Benedict became the most outstanding pope of the eighteenth century and favored the Passionists, "the smallest mustard seed in the church" according to Paul, and struggling to survive.

ST. PAUL OF THE CROSS

"When I received the news of his election, although I had never known him as cardinal, I felt in my heart an extraordinary movement, never before experienced at such an event, which aroused such lively hope in me that he would be the holy and zealous shepherd who would provide for a spirituality so much forgotten in Christendom. My spirit broke out in praise and thanksgiving for the mercy God has shown his people" (Letter 266, January 10, 1741).

PRAYER

Help us see signs like those you saw, Lord,
signs so small they may be missed.
Yes, signs are there:
Sometimes it's an outsider
whom we never expected to help us at all.
Sometimes it's unexpected,
something we never thought about before.
Often it's as small as Bread.

You are the God who works great wonders
by sending us simple signs,
words, things that seem like nothing.
Amen.

GOSPEL

Jesus went to the Mount of Olives. But early in the morning he arrived again in the temple area, and all the people started coming to him, and he sat down and taught them. Then the scribes and the Pharisees brought a woman who had been caught in adultery and made her stand in the middle. They said to him, "Teacher, this woman was caught in the very act of committing adultery. Now in the law, Moses commanded us to stone such women. So what do you say?" They said this to test him, so that they could have some charge to bring against him. Jesus bent down and began to write on the ground with his finger. But when they continued asking him, he straightened up and said to them, "Let the one among you who is without sin be the first to throw a stone at her." Again he bent down and wrote on the ground. And in response, they went away one by one, beginning with the elders. So he was left alone with the woman before him. Then Jesus straightened up and said to her, "Woman, where are they? Has no one condemned you?" She replied, "No one, sir." Then Jesus said, "Neither do I condemn you. Go, and from now on do not sin any more."

JOHN 8: 1-11

REFLECTION

The story of the woman accused of adultery takes place in the temple area during the Feast of the Tabernacles when Jesus proclaimed himself the light of the world and living water bringing life. His enemies fiercely disputed his claims. Did they introduce the woman to discredit him? Earlier, he said "As I hear, I judge, and my judgment is just" (Jn 5:30). Here was a test.

Moses, according to the woman's accusers, commanded she be stoned. What is his judgment?

From our perspective today adultery—which is still wrong—is not the only issue here. Gender injustice is also at stake. The woman was treated badly by men. Where is the man in the case?

Then, Jewish religious law said that if a woman were caught in the act of adultery and two men witnessed it, she could be stoned to death or strangled. The system led to abuse, historians say; two witnesses paid by a vengeful husband or a husband who wanted to get rid of his wife, might give false testimony and have her stoned to death.

The Word made flesh brings a lens of justice and mercy to every age and in the temple that day, the woman received life and light from him. Her accusers also were struck by the judgment of Jesus. We believe he offers that same light for knowing what is right and just today to all of us.

From the time of his spiritual conversion as a young man, Paul of the Cross was particularly conscious of God's grace enabling him to know himself. It made him see himself, his motives, his weaknesses. He called himself "a miracle of God's infinite mercy."

ST. PAUL OF THE CROSS

"During the day I had a special knowledge of myself. I know that I told my Divine Savior that I could call myself nothing other than a miracle of his infinite mercy" (Spiritual Diary, December 28, 1720).

PRAYER

Lord,
let me judge others with your eyes, your heart and your mind.
Help me work for a world that is right and just,
But give me first the grace to know myself.
Amen.

GOSPEL

Jesus went to the Mount of Olives. But early in the morning he arrived again in the temple area, and all the people started coming to him, and he sat down and taught them. Then the scribes and the Pharisees brought a woman who had been caught in adultery and made her stand in the middle. They said to him, "Teacher, this woman was caught in the very act of committing adultery. Now in the law, Moses commanded us to stone such women. So what do you say?" They said this to test him, so that they could have some charge to bring against him. Jesus bent down and began to write on the ground with his finger. But when they continued asking him, he straightened up and said to them, "Let the one among you who is without sin be the first to throw a stone at her." Again he bent down and wrote on the ground. And in response, they went away one by one, beginning with the elders. So he was left alone with the woman before him. Then Jesus straightened up and said to her, "Woman, where are they? Has no one condemned you?" She replied, "No one, sir." Then Jesus said, "Neither do I condemn you. Go, and from now on do not sin any more."

JOHN 8: 1-11

REFLECTION

When we read this story about the woman caught in adultery and brought to Jesus, who is asked if she should be stoned to death, our usual reaction is: "That's barbaric!"

And it is. We shudder to think that in some parts of the world stoning to death still takes place. And it does.

"Choose life," we're told in Lent. That's what Jesus did in the case of the woman. He obviously did not condemn her to death when he bent down to write his mysterious message on the ground, a message that drove her accusers away. "Has no one condemned you, woman? Neither do I."

141

But still we, as a society, have far to go to respect human life from birth to death. We still seem to prefer war and violence to patient persuasion and negotiation. We condone abortion. We punish crime instead of trying to rehabilitate the criminal.

The passion of Jesus is the ultimate call to respect life. In the callous disregard of Pilate, the brutality of the soldiers, the conniving of the chief priests and leaders of the people, the desertion of his friends, we have a powerful warning: Choose life. Care for it and cherish it. Life is a gift of God.

During his ministry of over forty years, St. Paul of the Cross preached over 250 missions in south-central Italy. Among those attracted to him were bandits who roamed the roads and swamp lands intent on robbery and plunder. Paul was instrumental in re-uniting many of these men with their families and society. He saw life in them when others saw death. He urged preachers of God's word to bring life to others in their preaching:

ST. PAUL OF THE CROSS

"So many wanted to confess to him, not only important people, but the least, the fiercest souls, beggars, the poorest, because he showed all a special charity. Like a compassionate doctor, he cared for those in most need. He used to say that bandits and people like them were his greatest friends, and they seeing his love, became strongly attached to him." (The Life of Blessed Paul, by St. Vincent Strambi, Chapter 14)

PRAYER

Father,
Creator of all and Giver of life,
The smallest and largest of your creatures
live because of you.
We are blessed by your many gifts.
and thank you for your blessings.
Help us care for life
in all its many forms.
Amen.

In Year C, when the preceding Gospel is read on Sunday, the following text is used.

GOSPEL

Jesus spoke to them again, saying, "I am the light of the world. Whoever follows me will not walk in darkness, but will have the light of life." So the Pharisees said to him, "You testify on your own behalf, so your testimony cannot be verified." Jesus answered and said to them, "Even if I do testify on my own behalf, my testimony can be verified, because I know where I came from and where I am going. But you do not know where I come from or where I am going. You judge by appearances, but I do not judge anyone. And even if I should judge, my judgment is valid, because I am not alone, but it is I and the Father who sent me. Even in your law it is written that the testimony of two men can be verified. I testify on my behalf and so does the Father who sent me." So they said to him, "Where is your father?" Jesus answered, "You know neither me nor my Father. If you knew me, you would know my Father also." He spoke these words while teaching in the treasury in the temple area. But no one arrested him, because his hour had not yet come.

JOHN 8: 12-20

REFLECTION

John's Gospel continues to report Jesus' teaching in the temple area during the Feast of Tabernacles. The feast, also called Succoth, was an ancient harvest feast, but it also recalled God's presence as the Jews journeyed through the desert from Egypt to the Promised Land. God provided a pillar of cloud by day and a fiery light by night to guide them on their way. A great fire was lit in the temple during the feast.

"I am the light of the world," Jesus cried out, "Whoever follows me will not walk in darkness, but will have the light of life." His opponents opposed his claims, which make him like God, and demanded proof.

"I testify on my behalf and so does the Father who sent me," Jesus replies. His own life is witness to who he is; and his Father witnesses to him too.

Do our lives witness to who we are? It's not just words or dreams or desires, but our lives that witness. As members of his Body, we have a high goal: to bring life to the world. "You are the light of the world," Jesus says in Matthew's Gospel.

And doesn't our witness to Jesus also mean sharing in the mystery of his cross? This was the goal St. Paul of the Cross set.

ST. PAUL OF THE CROSS

"When shall we imitate more perfectly that dear Savior who emptied himself? When shall we become so humble as to be a 'reproach among men and an outcast among the people?' When shall we become like little babies clinging to the breast of Jesus, our Spouse, Father and Protector? . . . When, oh when? Please ask the Lord to grant us this grace" (Letter 11, August 29, 1726).

PRAYER

Lord Jesus,
is imitating you beyond us?
How can we be light of the world, like you?
Let your light guide our steps
and unite us to you,
Help us be witnesses to your cross
and follow you to your kingdom.
Amen.

GOSPEL

JESUS SAID TO THE PHARISEES:

"I am going away and you will look for me, but you will die in your sin. Where I am going you cannot come." So the Jews said, "He is not going to kill himself, is he, because he said, 'Where I am going you cannot come'?" He said to them, "You belong to what is below, I belong to what is above. You belong to this world, but I do not belong to this world. That is why I told you that you will die in your sins. For if you do not believe that I AM, you will die in your sins." So they said to him, "Who are you?" Jesus said to them, "What I told you from the beginning. I have much to say about you in condemnation. But the one who sent me is true, and what I heard from him I tell the world." They did not realize that he was speaking to them of the Father. So Jesus said to them, "When you lift up the Son of Man, then you will realize that I AM, and that I do nothing on my own, but I say only what the Father taught me. The one who sent me is with me. He has not left me alone, because I always do what is pleasing to him." Because he spoke this way, many came to believe in him.

JOHN 8: 21-30

REFLECTION

Once again, our Gospel reports what Jesus said in the temple area during the Feast of Tabernacles. His urgent words address especially those who oppose him. The time is short; the Light that guides the world has appeared, but Jesus "is going away" and those who reject him will die in their sins.

We're not detached observers of a time long ago, as we listen to this Gospel, watching others challenged to believe. The challenge is not just to someone else; we're challenged ourselves to answer the question: Who is Jesus Christ?

He is "I AM," a divine title his enemies find blasphemous, but believers find true. In Hebrew it means "He who is always there." Later in John's Gospel, Thomas bows before Jesus and says "My Lord and my God," for he recognizes that the One lifted up on the cross is indeed "I AM."

Our Gospel calls us to reverence the One lifted up on the Cross as the days of Holy Week approach. He is "I AM," true God, sent by the Father, "who so loved the world that he sent his only Son." And he will always be there.

In an early letter to Bishop Count Peter Garangi, who worked to establish the Passionists as a new congregation in the church, St. Paul of the Cross emphasized the importance of the mystery of the passion and death of Jesus as a revelation of God.

ST. PAUL OF THE CROSS

"So many believers live in forgetfulness of how much our Divine Savior did and suffered; they sleep in a swamp of evil. We need zealous workers to awaken them from their sleep in darkness and the shadow of death by the trumpet of God's word and by meditating on the Passion of Jesus Christ, so that God be glorified by many who will be converted and pray and lead a holy life" (Letter 266, January 10, 1741).

PRAYER

Lord Jesus Christ,
Draw me to your cross
and show me your wounds, your bitter death,
   your triumph over the tomb.
God with us, always there,
God who shares our humanity,
God who loves us so much,
keep me in mind of you,
save me from forgetfulness.
Amen.

GOSPEL

Jesus said to those Jews who believed in him, "If you remain in my word, you will truly be my disciples, and you will know the truth, and the truth will set you free." They answered him, "We are descendants of Abraham and have never been enslaved to anyone. How can you say, 'You will become free'?" Jesus answered them, "Amen, amen, I say to you, everyone who commits sin is a slave of sin. A slave does not remain in a household forever, but a son always remains. So if the Son frees you, then you will truly be free. I know that you are descendants of Abraham. But you are trying to kill me, because my word has no room among you. I tell you what I have seen in the Father's presence; then do what you have heard from the Father."

They answered and said to him, "Our father is Abraham." Jesus said to them, "If you were Abraham's children, you would be doing the works of Abraham. But now you are trying to kill me, a man who has told you the truth that I heard from God; Abraham did not do this. You are doing the works of your father!" So they said to him, "We were not born of fornication. We have one Father, God." Jesus said to them, "If God were your Father, you would love me, for I came from God and am here; I did not come on my own, but he sent me."

JOHN 8: 31-42

REFLECTION

Those listening to Jesus teaching in the temple area claim that they're "descendants of Abraham." As they look at the splendid buildings of the temple, its well-ordered worship, the structures of ancient tradition known to them so well, they probably ask, Why listen to this man? They have the promises God made to Abraham; the temple and its majestic rites are a pledge of it. God's promises are automatically theirs.

But God's promises are not automatic. Jesus replies, "If you were the children of Abraham you would be doing the works of Abraham." The great patriarch was a nomad who accepted truth as it was revealed and moved from place to place. He discovered the works of God from within.

It's good to remember that John's Gospel was written well after the temple and Jerusalem itself had been destroyed by the Romans in 70 AD. Who were the "descendants of Abraham" then? Were they Jews and Jewish-Christians longing for the restoration and comfort of those ancient structures gone away? Are they being reminded in this Gospel that Abraham, our father in faith, ventured out into paths unknown, and One greater than Abraham now leads them?

In fast moving times like ours, this Gospel may offer the same lesson. Are we being called to have faith like Abraham's, a mystic faith that looks for light within? Two centuries ago, Paul of the Cross faced changing times by strongly urging those who sought his advice to center themselves in the unchanging One we meet "in spirit and truth." God within is our teacher.

ST. PAUL OF THE CROSS

"Jesus will teach you. I don't want you to indulge in vain imagery over this. Leave yourself free to take flight and rest in the Supreme Good, all consumed by fire, absorbed, beside itself and in admiration of the divine perfections, especially at the Infinite Goodness which made itself so small within our humanity" (Letter 18, December 30, 1730).

PRAYER

O God, you are my God,
For you I long.
My body pines for you,
Like a dry, weary land without water (Psalm 63).
Amen.

GOSPEL

JESUS SAID TO THE JEWS:

"Amen, amen, I say to you, whoever keeps my word will never see death." So the Jews said to him, "Now we are sure that you are possessed. Abraham died, as did the prophets, yet you say, 'Whoever keeps my word will never taste death.' Are you greater than our father Abraham, who died? Or the prophets, who died? Who do you make yourself out to be?" Jesus answered, "If I glorify myself, my glory is worth nothing; but it is my Father who glorifies me, of whom you say, 'He is our God.' You do not know him, but I know him. And if I should say that I do not know him, I would be like you a liar. But I do know him and I keep his word. Abraham your father rejoiced to see my day; he saw it and was glad." So the Jews said to him, "You are not yet fifty years old and you have seen Abraham?" Jesus said to them, "Amen, amen, I say to you, before Abraham came to be, I AM." So they picked up stones to throw at him; but Jesus hid and went out of the temple area.

JOHN 8: 51-59

REFLECTION

The previous four of our Lenten Gospels recorded Jesus' words during the Feast of Tabernacles in the temple area. It was hardly a public square, an open space where you could say anything; certainly not the freer space of Galilee or other places where Jesus taught and did great works.

The temple area was under the tight control of the Jewish authorities and his audience was often hostile, as John's Gospel indicates. At times, they cry out to arrest him and they pick up stones to kill him.

Yet, Jesus will not be silenced. "Amen, amen, I say to you, before Abraham came to be, I AM," he says to them. He proclaims fearlessly his divine status: "I am always there."

Are we fearless enough to tell his story, to repeat his message, to proclaim him everywhere, even where he and his works are rejected? "I know him," Jesus says about his Father, "and if I should say that I do not know him, I would be like you a liar. But I do know him and I keep his word."

The world today, especially our western world, can be hostile to Jesus Christ. Are we brave enough to witness where his name is ridiculed or ignored?

The eighteenth century world of Paul of the Cross surely wasn't the same as ours, but wouldn't this zealous man, if he were alive today, be a zealous witness to Jesus Christ? He exhausted himself preaching the Gospel in the poor, unhealthy swamplands of the Tuscan Maremma. What would he do now? Zeal always finds a way. "The love of God is ingenious," he used to say

ST. PAUL OF THE CROSS

"Today I am leaving for a mission amidst fierce storms. But no matter— it's for God's glory. You should accompany me with fervent prayers for the conversion of souls" (Letter 18, December 30, 1730).

PRAYER

Lord Jesus,
you spoke the truth,
even when others rejected your word.
Make me a zealous witness,
not fearing to speak your name
wherever I may be,
and help me live according to your teaching.
Amen.

GOSPEL

The Jews picked up rocks to stone Jesus. Jesus answered them, "I have shown you many good works from my Father. For which of these are you trying to stone me?" The Jews answered him, "We are not stoning you for a good work but for blasphemy. You, a man, are making yourself God." Jesus answered them, "Is it not written in your law, 'I said, "You are gods"'? If it calls them gods to whom the word of God came, and Scripture cannot be set aside, can you say that the one whom the Father has consecrated and sent into the world blasphemes because I said, 'I am the Son of God'? If I do not perform my Father's works, do not believe me; but if I perform them, even if you do not believe me, believe the works, so that you may realize and understand that the Father is in me and I am in the Father." Then they tried again to arrest him; but he escaped from their power.

He went back across the Jordan to the place where John first baptized, and there he remained. Many came to him and said, "John performed no sign, but everything John said about this man was true." And many there began to believe in him.

JOHN 10: 31-42

REFLECTION

Jesus came again to Jerusalem for another feast, the Feast of the Dedication of the Temple, John's Gospel says. It's a feast celebrated sometime in late November to late December, recalling the rededication of the temple after its profanation by Antiochus Epiphanes in the second century BC.

The Jewish feasts are signs in John's Gospel that reveal who Jesus is; they inspire his words and the miracles he does. In fact, he replaces them. On the Sabbath, (chapter 5) he heals the paralyzed man at the pool at Bethsaida. The Son will not rest from giving life as the Father never rests from giving life. On the Passover (chapter 6), he is the true Bread from heaven, the manna that feeds multitudes. On the Feast of Tabernacles (chapters 7–9) he calls himself the light of the world and living water. On the Feast of the Dedication, he reveals himself as the true temple, the One who dwells among us and makes God's glory known.

Once more, Jesus proclaims in today's Gospel his relationship to the Father, "the Father is in me and I am in the Father." Yet, once more hostile listeners do not see the signs and accuse him of blasphemy, trying to stone him or have him arrested. But Jesus evades them and goes back across the Jordan to the place where John baptized and "many there began to believe in him."

So many signs are given to us. We have the scriptures, the sacraments, the witness of the saints. How tragic not to follow them to the Word made flesh!

ST. PAUL OF THE CROSS

"To maintain this divine friendship, frequent the sacraments, namely confession and holy Communion. When you approach the altar do so for this one reason alone, to let your soul be melted more and more in the fire of divine love. Remember that you are dealing with the holiest action that we can perform. How could our dear Jesus have done more than to give himself to be our food! Therefore let us love him who loves us. Let us be deeply devoted to the Blessed Sacrament. In church we should tremble with reverential awe" (Letter 8, February 21, 1722).

PRAYER

Lead me on, O Lord,
Through your holy signs,
through them, let me come to you.
Amen.

GOSPEL

Many of the Jews who had come to Mary and seen what Jesus had done began to believe in him. But some of them went to the Pharisees and told them what Jesus had done. So the chief priests and the Pharisees convened the Sanhedrin and said, "What are we going to do? This man is performing many signs. If we leave him alone, all will believe in him, and the Romans will come and take away both our land and our nation." But one of them, Caiaphas, who was high priest that year, said to them, "You know nothing, nor do you consider that it is better for you that one man should die instead of the people, so that the whole nation may not perish." He did not say this on his own, but since he was high priest for that year, he prophesied that Jesus was going to die for the nation, and not only for the nation, but also to gather into one the dispersed children of God. So from that day on they planned to kill him.

So Jesus no longer walked about in public among the Jews, but he left for the region near the desert, to a town called Ephraim, and there he remained with his disciples.

Now the Passover of the Jews was near, and many went up from the country to Jerusalem before Passover to purify themselves. They looked for Jesus and said to one another as they were in the temple area, "What do you think? That he will not come to the feast?"

JOHN 11: 45-56

REFLECTION

The reading today follows the story of Lazarus read on the fifth Sunday of Lent (A). The Resurrection of Lazarus, John's Gospel says, led the Jewish leaders to meet about the threat of political instability they saw Jesus bringing to their nation. It blinds them to everything else Jesus said or did. Even before he goes up to Jerusalem for the feast of the Passover, they have decided his fate. Their meeting anticipates the meeting of the Sanhedrin the night before his passion.

Political reasons are primary in the high priest Caiaphas's strong intervention. He's afraid of Rome's powerful reaction, so what does it matter if an innocent man, with no political ambitions dies? But for God it matters and God always sees that evil loses to good. With his usual taste for irony, John lets the high priest's own words express God's sovereign purpose: "he prophesied that Jesus was going to die for the nation, and not only for the nation, but also to gather into one the dispersed children of God."

The passion and Resurrection of Jesus is God's great sign that good triumphs over evil. God has the last word and, difficult as it is, we're called to believe in his power to triumph over evil, however invincible or entrenched it is in our world and in our lives.

Mystics like Paul of the Cross firmly believed in God's power to reverse evil and turn things to the good, and they strengthened that vision through meditation on the passion of Jesus. It was a source of courageous patience for them and it's still the same for us.

ST. PAUL OF THE CROSS

"Just as our dear Jesus willed his life here on earth to be ever spent in the midst of hardships, labors, privations, anguish, scorn, calumnies, thorns and the cruel death of the cross, so he made me realize that in embracing him, I must live my life in the midst of suffering. And oh, with what joy did my poor soul embrace every kind of hardship!" (Letter 51, August 29, 1737).

PRAYER

Lord, I thank you for dying on the cross
and bringing life to the world.
Amen.

HOLY
WEEK

GOSPEL

AT THE PROCESSION WITH PALMS

When Jesus and the disciples drew near Jerusalem and came to Bethphage on the Mount of Olives, Jesus sent two disciples, saying to them, "Go into the village opposite you, and immediately you will find an ass tethered, and a colt with her. Untie them and bring them here to me. And if anyone should say anything to you, reply, 'The master has need of them.' Then he will send them at once." This happened so that what had been spoken through the prophet might be fulfilled: / *Say to daughter Zion, / "Behold, your king comes to you, / meek and riding on an ass, / and on a colt, the foal of a beast of burden."* / The disciples went and did as Jesus had ordered them. They brought the ass and the colt and laid their cloaks over them, and he sat upon them. The very large crowd spread their cloaks on the road, while others cut branches from the trees and strewed them on the road. The crowds preceding him and those following kept crying out and saying: / "Hosanna to the Son of David; / blessed is the he who comes in the name of the Lord; / hosanna in the highest." / And when he entered Jerusalem the whole city was shaken and asked, "Who is this?" And the crowds replied, "This is Jesus the prophet, from Nazareth in Galilee."

MATTHEW 21: 1-11

GOSPEL

MASS

One of the Twelve, who was called Judas Iscariot, went to the chief priests and said, "What are you willing to give me if I hand him over to you?" They paid him thirty pieces of silver, and from that time on he looked for an opportunity to hand him over.

On the first day of the Feast of Unleavened Bread, the disciples approached Jesus and said, "Where do you want us to prepare for you to eat the Passover?" He said, "Go into the city to a certain man and tell him, 'The teacher says, "My appointed time draws near; in your house I shall celebrate the Passover with my disciples."'"The disciples then did as Jesus had ordered, and prepared the Passover.

When it was evening, he reclined at table with the Twelve. And while they were eating, he said, "Amen, I say to you, one of you will betray me." Deeply distressed at this, they began to say to him one after another, "Surely it is not I, Lord?" He said in reply, "He who has dipped his hand into the dish with me is the one who will betray me. The Son of Man indeed goes, as it is written of him, but woe to that man by whom the Son of Man is betrayed. It would be better for that man if he had never been born." Then Judas, his betrayer, said in reply, "Surely it is not I, Rabbi?" He answered, "You have said so."

While they were eating, Jesus took bread, said the blessing, broke it, and giving it to his disciples said, "Take and eat; this is my body." Then he took a cup, gave thanks, and gave it to them, saying, "Drink from it, all of you, for this is my blood of the covenant, which will be shed on behalf of many for the forgiveness of sins. I tell you, from now on I shall not drink this fruit of the vine until the day when I drink it with you new in the kingdom of my Father." Then, after singing a hymn, they went out to the Mount of Olives.

Then Jesus said to them, "This night all of you will have your faith in me shaken, for it is written: / *I will strike the shepherd, / and the sheep of the flock will be dispersed; /* but after I have been raised up, I shall go before you to Galilee." Peter said to him in reply, "Though all may have their faith in you shaken, mine will never be." Jesus said to him, "Amen, I say to you, this very night before the cock crows, you will deny me three times." Peter said to him, "Even though I should have to die with you, I will not deny you." And all the disciples spoke likewise.

Then Jesus came with them to a place called Gethsemane, and he said to his disciples, "Sit here while I go over there and pray." He took along Peter and the two sons of Zebedee, and began to feel sorrow and distress. Then he said to them, "My soul is sorrowful even to death. Remain here and keep watch with me." He advanced a little and fell prostrate in prayer, saying, "My Father, if it is possible, let this cup pass from me; yet, not as I will, but as you will." When he returned to his disciples he found them asleep. He said to Peter, "So you could not keep watch with me for one hour? Watch and pray that you may not undergo the test. The spirit is willing, but the flesh is weak." Withdrawing a second time, he prayed again, "My Father, if it is not possible that this cup pass without my drinking it, your will be done!" Then he returned once more and found them asleep, for they could not keep their eyes open. He left them and withdrew again and prayed a third time, saying the same thing again. Then he returned to his disciples and said to them, "Are you still sleeping and taking your rest? Behold, the hour is at hand when the Son of Man is to be handed over to sinners. Get up, let us go. Look, my betrayer is at hand."

While he was still speaking, Judas, one of the Twelve, arrived, accompanied by a large crowd, with swords and clubs, who had come from the chief priests and the elders of the people. His betrayer had arranged a sign with them, saying, "The man I shall kiss is the one; arrest him." Immediately he went over to Jesus and said, "Hail, Rabbi!" and he kissed him. Jesus answered him, "Friend, do what you have come for." Then stepping forward they laid hands on Jesus and arrested him. And behold, one of those who accompanied Jesus put his hand to his sword, drew it, and struck the high priest's servant, cutting off his ear. Then Jesus said to him, "Put your sword back into its sheath, for all who take the sword will perish by the sword. Do you think that I cannot call upon my Father and he will not provide me at this moment with more than twelve legions of angels? But then how would the Scriptures be fulfilled which say that it must come to pass in this way?" At that hour Jesus said to the crowds, "Have you come out as against a robber, with swords and clubs to seize me? Day after day I sat teaching in the temple area, yet you did not arrest me. But all this has come to pass that the writings of the prophets may be fulfilled." Then all the disciples left him and fled.

Those who had arrested Jesus led him away to Caiaphas the high priest, where the scribes and the elders were assembled. Peter was following him at a distance as far as the high priest's courtyard, and going inside he sat down with the servants to see the outcome. The chief priests and the entire Sanhedrin kept trying to obtain false testimony against Jesus in order to put him to death, but they found none, though many false witnesses came forward. Finally two came forward who stated, "This man said, 'I can destroy the temple of God and within three days rebuild it.'" The high priest rose and addressed him, "Have you no answer? What are these men testifying against you?" But Jesus was silent. Then the high priest said to him, "I order you to tell us under oath before the living God whether you are the Christ, the Son of God." Jesus said to him in reply, "You have said so. But I tell you: / From now on you will see 'the Son of Man / seated at the right hand of the Power' / and 'coming on the clouds of heaven.'" / Then the high priest tore his robes and said, "He has blasphemed! What further need have we of witnesses? You have now heard the blasphemy; what is your opinion?" They said in reply, "He deserves to die!" Then they spat in his face and struck him, while some slapped him, saying, "Prophesy for us, Christ: who is it that struck you?"

Now Peter was sitting outside in the courtyard. One of the maids came over to him and said, "You too were with Jesus the Galilean." But he denied it in front of everyone, saying, "I do not know what you are talking about!" As he went out to the gate, another girl saw him and said to those who were there, "This man was with Jesus the Nazorean." Again he denied it with an oath, "I do not know the man!" A little later the bystanders came over and said to Peter, "Surely you too are one of them; even your speech gives you away." At that he began to curse and to swear, "I do not know the man." And immediately a cock crowed. Then Peter remembered the word that Jesus had spoken: "Before the cock crows you will deny me three times." He went out and began to weep bitterly.

When it was morning, all the chief priests and the elders of the people took counsel against Jesus to put him to death. They bound him, led him away, and handed him over to Pilate, the governor.

Then Judas, his betrayer, seeing that Jesus had been condemned, deeply regretted what he had done. He returned the thirty pieces of silver to the chief priests and elders, saying, "I have sinned in betraying innocent blood." They said, "What is that to us? Look to it yourself." Flinging the money into the temple, he departed and went off and hanged himself. The chief priests gathered up the money, but said, "It is not lawful to deposit this in the temple treasury, for it is the price of blood." After consultation, they used it to buy the potter's field as a burial place for foreigners. That is why that field even today is called the Field of Blood. Then was fulfilled what had been said through Jeremiah the prophet, *And they took the thirty pieces of silver, the value of a man with a price on his head, a price set by some of the Israelites, and they paid it out for the potter's field just as the Lord had commanded me.*

Now Jesus stood before the governor, who questioned him, "Are you the king of the Jews?" Jesus said, "You say so." And when he was accused by the chief priests and elders, he made no answer. Then Pilate said to him, "Do you not hear how many things they are testifying against you?" But he did not answer him one word, so that the governor was greatly amazed.

Now on the occasion of the feast the governor was accustomed to release to the crowd one prisoner whom they wished. And at that time they had a notorious prisoner called Barabbas. So when they had assembled, Pilate said to them, "Which one do you want me to release to you, Barabbas, or Jesus called Christ?" For he knew that it was out of envy that they had handed him over. While he was still seated on the bench, his wife sent him a message, "Have nothing to do with that righteous man. I suffered much in a dream today because of him." The chief priests and the elders persuaded the crowds to ask for Barabbas but to destroy Jesus. The governor said to them in reply, "Which of the two do you want me to release to you?" They answered, "Barabbas!" Pilate said to them, "Then what shall I do with Jesus called Christ?" They all said, "Let him be crucified!" But he said, "Why? What evil has he done?" They only shouted the louder, "Let him be crucified!" When Pilate saw that he was not succeeding at all, but that a riot was breaking out instead, he took water and washed his hands in the sight of the crowd, saying, "I am innocent of this man's blood. Look to it yourselves." And the whole people said in reply, "His blood be upon us and upon our children." Then he released Barabbas to them, but after he had Jesus scourged, he handed him over to be crucified.

Then the soldiers of the governor took Jesus inside the praetorium and gathered the whole cohort around him. They stripped off his clothes and threw a scarlet military cloak about him. Weaving a crown out of thorns, they placed it on his head, and a reed in his right hand. And kneeling before him, they mocked him, saying, "Hail, King of the Jews!" They spat upon him and took the reed and kept striking him on the head. And when they had mocked him, they stripped him of the cloak, dressed him in his own clothes, and led him off to crucify him.

As they were going out, they met a Cyrenian named Simon; this man they pressed into service to carry his cross.

And when they came to a place called Golgotha — which means Place of the Skull —, they gave Jesus wine to drink mixed with gall. But when he had tasted it, he refused to drink. After they had crucified him, they divided his garments by casting lots; then they sat down and kept watch over him there. And they placed over his head the written charge against him: This is Jesus, the King of the Jews. Two revolutionaries were crucified with him, one on his right and the other on his left. Those passing by reviled him, shaking their heads and saying, "You who would destroy the temple and rebuild it in three days, save yourself, if you are the Son of God, and come down from the cross!" Likewise the chief priests with the scribes and elders mocked him and said, "He saved others; he cannot save himself. So he is the king of Israel! Let him come down from the cross now, and we will believe in him. He trusted in God; let him deliver him now if he wants him. For he said, 'I am the Son of God.'" The revolutionaries who were crucified with him also kept abusing him in the same way.

From noon onward, darkness came over the whole land until three in the afternoon. And about three o'clock Jesus cried out in a loud voice, *"Eli, Eli, lema sabachthani?"* which means, "My God, my God, why have you forsaken me?" Some of the bystanders who heard it said, "This one is calling for Elijah." Immediately one of them ran to get a sponge; he soaked it in wine, and putting it on a reed, gave it to him to drink. But the rest said, "Wait, let us see if Elijah comes to save him." But Jesus cried out again in a loud voice, and gave up his spirit.

Here all kneel and pause for a short time.

And behold, the veil of the sanctuary was torn in two from top to bottom. The earth quaked, rocks were split, tombs were opened, and the bodies of many saints who had fallen asleep were raised. And coming forth from their tombs after his resurrection, they entered the holy city and appeared to many. The centurion and the men with him who were keeping watch over Jesus feared greatly when they saw the earthquake and all that was happening, and they said, "Truly, this was the Son of God!" There were many women there, looking on from a distance, who had followed Jesus from Galilee, ministering to him. Among them were Mary Magdalene and Mary the mother of James and Joseph, and the mother of the sons of Zebedee.

When it was evening, there came a rich man from Arimathea named Joseph, who was himself a disciple of Jesus. He went to Pilate and asked for the body of Jesus; then Pilate ordered it to be handed over. Taking the body, Joseph wrapped it in clean linen and laid it in his new tomb that he had hewn in the rock. Then he rolled a huge stone across the entrance to the tomb and departed. But Mary Magdalene and the other Mary remained sitting there, facing the tomb.

The next day, the one following the day of preparation, the chief priests and the Pharisees gathered before Pilate and said, "Sir, we remember that this impostor while still alive said, 'After three days I will be raised up.' Give orders, then, that the grave be secured until the third day, lest his disciples come and steal him and say to the people, 'He has been raised from the dead.' This last imposture would be worse than the first." Pilate said to them, "The guard is yours; go, secure it as best you can." So they went and secured the tomb by fixing a seal to the stone and setting the guard.

MATTHEW 26: 14-75 & 27: 1-66

Shorter form: MATTHEW 27:11-54

REFLECTION

Matthew's story of the passion of Jesus is the first of the four Gospels we read in Holy Week. Why four? Because this story can't be expressed easily; each of the evangelists has something to say.

It's a story initially told by Jesus Christ after he rose from the dead. The Easter Gospels offer its first form. Appearing to his disciples at Jerusalem that day "Jesus came and stood among them and said, 'Peace be with you.' When he had said this, he showed them his hands and his side" (Jn 20:19–21). To his Emmaus disciples that same day, Jesus said: 'Was it not necessary that the Christ should suffer these things and enter into his glory?' And beginning with Moses and all the prophets, he interpreted to them in all the scriptures the things concerning himself" (Lk 24:26–27). The Gospel narratives today grew from this first telling by the Risen Christ.

The Passion of Jesus is an Easter story that brings hope. He did not hide his wounds; he showed them to his disciples. He doesn't dismiss his sufferings and death as an embarrassing setback; the power of God appeared in them. As Jesus revealed it, he made the hearts of his followers burn with rejoicing. Now he tells it to us and hopefully we respond with a simple response of love.

ST. PAUL OF THE CROSS

*"If you cannot meditate on the Passion of Jesus, speak about it to him:
"Lord so loving, what was within your heart in the garden? Such pain,
such blood, such a bitter agony! And all for me? At times, it will seem
you can neither meditate or remain lovingly attentive before God. You're
like a statue. Don't worry, continue to pray. Stir up your faith in God's
presence and go into him, lamenting like St. Augustine: 'O Beauty, ever
ancient, ever new, I sought you outside and I had you within.' We have a
treasure within."* (Letter 105, June 26, 1736).

PRAYER

May the Passion of Christ be always in our hearts!
Amen.

GOSPEL

PROCESSION WITH PALMS

When Jesus and his disciples drew near to Jerusalem, to Bethpage and Bethany at the Mount of Olives, he sent two of his disciples and said to them, "Go into the village opposite you, and immediately on entering it, you will find a colt tethered on which no one has ever sat. Untie it and bring it here. If anyone should say to you, 'Why are you doing this?' reply, 'The Master has need of it and will send it back here at once.'" So they went off and found a colt tethered at a gate outside on the street, and they untied it. Some of the bystanders said to them, "What are you doing, untying the colt?" They answered them just as Jesus had told them to, and they permitted them to do it. So they brought the colt to Jesus and put their cloaks over it. And he sat on it. Many people spread their cloaks on the road, and others spread leafy branches that they had cut from the fields. Those preceding him as well as those following kept crying out: / "Hosanna! / Blessed is he who comes in the name of the Lord! / Blessed is the kingdom of our father David that is to come! / Hosanna in the highest!"

MARK 11: 1-10

Alternative: JOHN 12:12-16

GOSPEL

MASS

The Passover and the Feast of Unleavened Bread were to take place in two days' time. So the chief priests and the scribes were seeking a way to arrest him by treachery and put him to death. They said, "Not during the festival, for fear that there may be a riot among the people."

When he was in Bethany reclining at table in the house of Simon the leper, a woman came with an alabaster jar of perfumed oil, costly genuine spikenard. She broke the alabaster jar and poured it on his head. There were some who were indignant. "Why has there been this waste of perfumed oil? It could have been sold for more than three hundred days' wages and the money given to the poor." They were infuriated with her. Jesus said, "Let her alone. Why do you make trouble for her? She has done a good thing for me. The poor you will always have with you, and whenever you wish you can do good to them, but you will not always have me. She has done what she could. She has anticipated anointing my body for burial. Amen, I say to you, wherever the gospel is proclaimed to the whole world, what she has done will be told in memory of her."

Then Judas Iscariot, one of the Twelve, went off to the chief priests to hand him over to them. When they heard him they were pleased and promised to pay him money. Then he looked for an opportunity to hand him over.

On the first day of the Feast of Unleavened Bread, when they sacrificed the Passover lamb, his disciples said to him, "Where do you want us to go and prepare for you to eat the Passover?" He sent two of his disciples and said to them, "Go into a city and a man will meet you, carrying a jar of water. Follow him. Wherever he enters, say to the master of the house, 'The Teacher says, "Where is my guest room where I may eat the Passover with my disciples?"' Then he will show you a large upper room furnished and ready. Make the preparations for us there." The disciples then went off, entered the city, and found it just as he had told them; and they prepared the Passover.

When it was evening, he came with the Twelve. And as they reclined at table and were eating, Jesus said, "Amen, I say to you, one of you will betray me, one who is eating with me." They began to be distressed and to say to him, one by one, "Surely it is not I?" He said to them, "One of the Twelve, the one who dips with me into the dish. For the Son of Man indeed goes, as it is written of him, but woe to that man by whom the Son of Man is betrayed. It would be better for that man if he had never been born."

While they were eating, he took bread, said the blessing, broke it, and gave it to them, and said, "Take it; this is my body." Then he took a cup, gave thanks, and gave it to them, and they all drank from it. He said to them, "This is my blood of the covenant, which will be shed for many. Amen, I say to you, I shall not drink again the fruit of the vine until the day when I drink it new in the kingdom of God." Then, after singing a hymn, they went out to the Mount of Olives.

Then Jesus said to them, "All of you will have your faith shaken, for it is written: / *I will strike the shepherd,* / *and the sheep will be dispersed.* / But after I have been raised up, I shall go before you to Galilee." Peter said to him, "Even though all should have their faith shaken, mine will not be." Then Jesus said to him, "Amen, I say to you, this very night before the cock crows twice you will deny me three times." But he vehemently replied, "Even though I should have to die with you, I will not deny you." And they all spoke similarly.

Then they came to a place named Gethsemane, and he said to his disciples, "Sit here while I pray." He took with him Peter, James and John, and began to be troubled and distressed. Then he said to them, "My soul is sorrowful even to death. Remain here and keep watch." He advanced a little and fell to the ground and prayed that if it were possible the hour might pass by him; he said, "Abba, Father, all things are possible to you. Take this cup away from me, but not what I will but what you will." When he returned he found them asleep. He said to Peter, "Simon, are you asleep? Could you not keep watch for one hour? Watch and pray that you may not undergo the test. The spirit is willing but the flesh is weak." Withdrawing again, he prayed, saying the same thing. Then he returned once more and found them asleep, for they could not keep their eyes open and did not know what to answer him. He returned a third time and said to them, "Are you still sleeping and taking your rest? It is enough. The hour has come. Behold, the Son of Man is to be handed over to sinners. Get up, let us go. See, my betrayer is at hand."

Then, while he was still speaking, Judas, one of the Twelve, arrived, accompanied by a crowd with swords and clubs who had come from the chief priests, the scribes, and the elders. His betrayer had arranged a signal with them, saying, "The man I shall kiss is the one; arrest him and lead him away securely." He came and immediately went over to him and said, "Rabbi." And he kissed him. At this they laid hands on him and arrested him. One of the bystanders drew his sword, struck the high priest's servant, and cut off his ear. Jesus said to them in reply, "Have you come out as against a robber, with swords and clubs, to seize me? Day after day I was with you teaching in the temple area, yet you did not arrest me; but that the Scriptures may be fulfilled." And they all left him and fled. Now a young man followed him wearing nothing but a linen cloth about his body. They seized him, but he left the cloth behind and ran off naked.

They led Jesus away to the high priest, and all the chief priests and the elders and the scribes came together. Peter followed him at a distance into the high priest's courtyard and was seated with the guards, warming himself at the fire. The chief priests and the entire Sanhedrin kept trying to obtain testimony against Jesus in order to put him to death, but they found none. Many gave false witness against him, but their testimony did not agree. Some took the stand and testified falsely against him, alleging, "We heard him say, 'I will destroy this temple made with hands and within three days I will build another not made with hands.'" Even so their testimony did not agree. The high priest rose before the assembly and questioned Jesus, saying, "Have you no answer? What are these men testifying against you?" But he was silent and answered nothing. Again the high priest asked him and said to him, "Are you the Christ, the son of the Blessed One?" Then Jesus answered, "I am; / and 'you will see the Son of Man / seated at the right hand of the Power / and coming with the clouds of heaven'." / At that the high priest tore his garments and said, "What further need have we of witnesses? You have heard the blasphemy. What do you think?" They all condemned him as deserving to die. Some began to spit on him. They blindfolded him and struck him and said to him, "Prophesy!" And the guards greeted him with blows.

While Peter was below in the courtyard, one of the high priest's maids came along. Seeing Peter warming himself, she looked intently at him and said, "You too were with the Nazarene, Jesus." But he denied it saying, "I neither know nor understand what you are talking about." So he went out into the outer court. Then the cock crowed. The maid saw him and began again to say to the bystanders, "This man is one of them." Once again he denied it. A little later the bystanders said to Peter once more, "Surely you are one of them; for you too are a Galilean." He began to curse and to swear, "I do not know this man about whom you are talking." And immediately a cock crowed a second time. Then Peter remembered the word that Jesus had said to him, "Before the cock crows twice you will deny me three times." He broke down and wept.

As soon as morning came, the chief priests with the elders and the scribes, that is, the whole Sanhedrin held a council. They bound Jesus, led him away, and handed him over to Pilate. Pilate questioned him, "Are you the king of the Jews?" He said to him in reply, "You say so." The chief priests accused him of many things. Again Pilate questioned him, "Have you no answer? See how many things they accuse you of." Jesus gave him no further answer, so that Pilate was amazed.

Now on the occasion of the feast he used to release to them one prisoner whom they requested. A man called Barabbas was then in prison along with the rebels who had committed murder in a rebellion. The crowd came forward and began to ask him to do for them as he was accustomed. Pilate answered, "Do you want me to release to you the king of the Jews?" For he knew that it was out of envy that the chief priests had handed him over. But the chief priests stirred up the crowd to have him release Barabbas for them instead. Pilate again said to them in reply, "Then what do you want me to do with the man you call the king of the Jews?" They shouted again, "Crucify him." Pilate said to them, "Why? What evil has he done?" They only shouted the louder, "Crucify him." So Pilate, wishing to satisfy the crowd, released Barabbas to them and, after he had Jesus scourged, handed him over to be crucified.

The soldiers led him away inside the palace, that is, the praetorium, and assembled the whole cohort. They clothed him in purple and, weaving a crown of thorns, placed it on him. They began to salute him with, "Hail, King of the Jews!" and kept striking his head with a reed and spitting upon him. They knelt before him in homage. And when they had mocked him, they stripped him of the purple cloak, dressed him in his own clothes, and led him out to crucify him.

They pressed into service a passer-by, Simon, a Cyrenian, who was coming in from the country, the father of Alexander and Rufus, to carry his cross.

They brought him to the place of Golgotha—which is translated Place of the Skull—. They gave him wine drugged with myrrh, but he did not take it. Then they crucified him and divided his garments by casting lots for them to see what each should take. It was nine o'clock in the morning when they crucified him. The inscription of the charge against him read, "The King of the Jews." With him they crucified two revolutionaries, one on his right and one on his left. Those passing by reviled him, shaking their heads and saying, "Aha! You who would destroy the temple and rebuild it in three days, save yourself by coming down from the cross." Likewise the chief priests, with the scribes, mocked him among themselves and said, "He saved others; he cannot save himself. Let the Christ, the King of Israel, come down now from the cross that we may see and believe." Those who were crucified with him also kept abusing him.

At noon darkness came over the whole land until three in the afternoon. And at three o'clock Jesus cried out in a loud voice, *"Eloi, Eloi, lema sabachthani?"* which is translated, "My God, my God, why have you forsaken me?" Some of the bystanders who heard it said, "Look, he is calling Elijah." One of them ran, soaked a sponge with wine, put it on a reed and gave it to him to drink saying, "Wait, let us see if Elijah comes to take him down." Jesus gave a loud cry and breathed his last.

Here all kneel and pause for a short time.

The veil of the sanctuary was torn in two from top to bottom. When the centurion who stood facing him saw how he breathed his last he said, "Truly this man was the Son of God!"

There were also women looking on from a distance. Among them were Mary Magdalene, Mary the mother of the younger James and of Joses, and Salome. These women had followed him when he was in Galilee and ministered to him. There were also many other women who had come up with him to Jerusalem.

When it was already evening, since it was the day of preparation, the day before the sabbath, Joseph of Arimathea, a distinguished member of the council, who was himself awaiting the kingdom of God, came and courageously went to Pilate and asked for the body of Jesus. Pilate was amazed that he was already dead. He summoned the centurion and asked him if Jesus had already died. And when he learned of it from the centurion, he gave the body to Joseph. Having bought a linen cloth, he took him down, wrapped him in the linen cloth, and laid him in a tomb that had been hewn out of the rock. Then he rolled a stone against the entrance to the tomb. Mary Magdalene and Mary the mother of Joses watched where he was laid.

MARK 14: 1-72 & 15: 1-47

Shorter form: MARK 15:1-39

REFLECTION

The Gospel of Mark, the first of the Gospels to appear in written form, presents Jesus going to death in utter desolation, draining the cup of suffering given him by his Father. His enemies viciously reject him; his disciples mostly betray him or desert him. Only a few remain as he goes on his way. His cry from the cross is a cry of faith mingled with deep fear and sorrow: "My God, my God, why have you forsaken me?"

As we read this Gospel, taut and fast-paced, we share with Jesus the dark mystery of unexplained suffering that all of us face in life. Yet, this mystery leads to life, a risen life.

The desolation Jesus experienced takes many forms, some quite hidden from what people see. Yes, the cross means physical pain, but suffering may also come from spiritual and psychological situations. Paul of the Cross spoke of this to a priest of his community who was experiencing the cross of spiritual desolation. God's grace would lift him up to bring life to someone else, the saint assured him. The mystery of the cross never ends in death.

ST. PAUL OF THE CROSS

"From what you tell me of your soul, I, with the little or no light that God gives me, tell you that the abandonment and desolation, and the rest you mention, are precisely preparing you for greater graces that will help you in the ministry for which his Divine Majesty has destined you either now or a some other time. Of that I have not doubt" (Letter 1217, September 13, 1759).

PRAYER

Lord,
let me hear joy and gladness,
let the bones you have crushed rejoice. . . .
Restore to me the joy of your salvation (Psalm 51).
Amen.

GOSPEL

PROCESSION WITH PALMS

Jesus proceeded on his journey up to Jerusalem. As he drew near to Bethpage and Bethany at the place called the Mount of Olives, he sent two of his disciples. He said, "Go into the village opposite you, and as you enter it you will find a colt tethered on which no one has ever sat. Untie it and bring it here. And if anyone should ask you, 'Why are you untying it?' you will answer, 'The Master has need of it.'" So those who had been sent went off and found everything just as he had told them. And as they were untying the colt, its owners said to them, "Why are you untying this colt?" They answered, "The Master has need of it." So they brought it to Jesus, threw their cloaks over the colt, and helped Jesus to mount. As he rode along, the people were spreading their cloaks on the road; and now as he was approaching the slope of the Mount of Olives, the whole multitude of his disciples began to praise God aloud with joy for all the mighty deeds they had seen. They proclaimed: / "Blessed is the king who comes / in the name of the Lord. / Peace in heaven / and glory in the highest." / Some of the Pharisees in the crowd said to him, "Teacher, rebuke your disciples." He said in reply, "I tell you, if they keep silent, the stones will cry out!"

LUKE 19: 28-40

GOSPEL

MASS

When the hour came, Jesus took his place at table with the apostles. He said to them, "I have eagerly desired to eat this Passover with you before I suffer, for, I tell you, I shall not eat it again until there is fulfillment in the kingdom of God." Then he took a cup, gave thanks, and said, "Take this and share it among yourselves; for I tell you that from this time on I shall not drink of the fruit of the vine until the kingdom of God comes." Then he took the bread, said the blessing, broke it, and gave it to them, saying, "This is my body, which will be given for you; do this in memory of me." And likewise the cup after they had eaten, saying, "This cup is the new covenant in my blood, which will be shed for you.

"And yet behold, the hand of the one who is to betray me is with me on the table; for the Son of Man indeed goes as it has been determined; but woe to that man by whom he is betrayed." And they began to debate among themselves who among them would do such a deed.

Then an argument broke out among them about which of them should be regarded as the greatest. He said to them, "The kings of the Gentiles lord it over them and those in authority over them are addressed as 'Benefactors'; but among you it shall not be so. Rather, let the greatest among you be as the youngest, and the leader as the servant. For who is greater: the one seated at table or the one who serves? Is it not the one seated at table? I am among you as the one who serves. It is you who have stood by me in my trials; and I confer a kingdom on you, just as my Father has conferred one on me, that you may eat and drink at my table in my kingdom; and you will sit on thrones judging the twelve tribes of Israel.

"Simon, Simon, behold Satan has demanded to sift all of you like wheat, but I have prayed that your own faith may not fail; and once you have turned back, you must strengthen your brothers." He said to him, "Lord, I am prepared to go to prison and to die with you." But he replied, "I tell you, Peter, before the cock crows this day, you will deny three times that you know me."

He said to them, "When I sent you forth without a money bag or a sack or sandals, were you in need of anything?" "No, nothing," they replied. He said to them, "But now one who has a money bag should take it, and likewise a sack, and one who does not have a sword should sell his cloak and buy one. For I tell you that this Scripture must be fulfilled in me, namely, *He was counted among the wicked;* and indeed what is written about me is coming to fulfillment." Then they said, "Lord, look, there are two swords here." But he replied, "It is enough!"

Then going out, he went, as was his custom, to the Mount of Olives, and the disciples followed him. When he arrived at the place he said to them, "Pray that you may not undergo the test." After withdrawing about a stone's throw from them and kneeling, he prayed, saying, "Father, if you are willing, take this cup away from me; still, not my will but yours be done." And to strengthen him an angel from heaven appeared to him. He was in such agony and he prayed so fervently that his sweat became like drops of blood falling on the ground. When he rose from prayer and returned to his disciples, he found them sleeping from grief. He said to them, "Why are you sleeping? Get up and pray that you may not undergo the test."

While he was still speaking, a crowd approached and in front was one of the Twelve, a man named Judas. He went up to Jesus to kiss him. Jesus said to him, "Judas, are you betraying the Son of Man with a kiss?" His disciples realized what was about to happen, and they asked, "Lord, shall we strike with a sword?" And one of them struck the high priest's servant and cut off his right ear. But Jesus said in reply, "Stop, no more of this!" Then he touched the servant's ear and healed him. And Jesus said to the chief priests and temple guards and elders who had come for him, "Have you come out as against a robber, with swords and clubs? Day after day I was with you in the temple area, and you did not seize me; but this is your hour, the time for the power of darkness."

After arresting him they led him away and took him into the house of the high priest; Peter was following at a distance. They lit a fire in the middle of the courtyard and sat around it, and Peter sat down with them. When a maid saw him seated in the light, she looked intently at him and said, "This man too was with him." But he denied it saying, "Woman, I do not know him." A short while later someone else saw him and said, "You too are one of them"; but Peter answered, "My friend, I am not." About an hour later, still another insisted, "Assuredly, this man too was with him, for he also is a Galilean." But Peter said, "My friend, I do not know what you are talking about." Just as he was saying this, the cock crowed, and the Lord turned and looked at Peter; and Peter remembered the word of the Lord, how he had said to him, "Before the cock crows today, you will deny me three times." He went out and began to weep bitterly. The men who held Jesus in custody were ridiculing and beating him. They blindfolded him and questioned him, saying, "Prophesy! Who is it that struck you?" And they reviled him in saying many other things against him.

When day came the council of elders of the people met, both chief priests and scribes, and they brought him before their Sanhedrin. They said, "If you are the Christ, tell us," but he replied to them, "If I tell you, you will not believe, and if I question, you will not respond. But from this time on the Son of Man will be seated at the right hand of the power of God." They all asked, "Are you then the Son of God?" He replied to them, "You say that I am." Then they said, "What further need have we for testimony? We have heard it from his own mouth."

Then the whole assembly of them arose and brought him before Pilate. They brought charges against him, saying, "We found this man misleading our people; he opposes the payment of taxes to Caesar and maintains that he is the Christ, a king." Pilate asked him, "Are you the king of the Jews?" He said to him in reply, "You say so." Pilate then addressed the chief priests and the crowds, "I find this man not guilty." But they were adamant and said, "He is inciting the people with his teaching throughout all Judea, from Galilee where he began even to here."

On hearing this Pilate asked if the man was a Galilean; and upon learning that he was under Herod's jurisdiction, he sent him to Herod, who was in Jerusalem at that time. Herod was very glad to see Jesus; he had been wanting to see him for a long time, for he had heard about him and had been hoping to see him perform some sign. He questioned him at length, but he gave him no answer. The chief priests and scribes, meanwhile, stood by accusing him harshly. Herod and his soldiers treated him contemptuously and mocked him, and after clothing him in resplendent garb, he sent him back to Pilate. Herod and Pilate became friends that very day, even though they had been enemies formerly. Pilate then summoned the chief priests, the rulers, and the people and said to them, "You brought this man to me and accused him of inciting the people to revolt. I have conducted my investigation in your presence and have not found this man guilty of the charges you have brought against him, nor did Herod, for he sent him back to us. So no capital crime has been committed by him. Therefore I shall have him flogged and then release him."

But all together they shouted out, "Away with this man! Release Barabbas to us." —Now Barabbas had been imprisoned for a rebellion that had taken place in the city and for murder.— Again Pilate addressed them, still wishing to release Jesus, but they continued their shouting, "Crucify him! Crucify him!" Pilate addressed them a third time, "What evil has this man done? I found him guilty of no capital crime. Therefore I shall have him flogged and then release him." With loud shouts, however, they persisted in calling for his crucifixion, and their voices prevailed. The verdict of Pilate was that their demand should be granted. So he released the man who had been imprisoned for rebellion and murder, for whom they asked, and he handed Jesus over to them to deal with as they wished.

As they led him away they took hold of a certain Simon, a Cyrenian, who was coming in from the country; and after laying the cross on him, they made him carry it behind Jesus. A large crowd of people followed Jesus, including many women who mourned and lamented him.

Jesus turned to them and said, "Daughters of Jerusalem, do not weep for me; weep instead for yourselves and for your children for indeed, the days are coming when people will say, 'Blessed are the barren, the wombs that never bore and the breasts that never nursed.' At that time people will say to the mountains, 'Fall upon us!' and to the hills, 'Cover us!' for if these things are done when the wood is green, what will happen when it is dry?" Now two others, both criminals, were led away with him to be executed.

When they came to the place called the Skull, they crucified him and the criminals there, one on his right, the other on his left. Then Jesus said, "Father, forgive them, they know not what they do." They divided his garments by casting lots. The people stood by and watched; the rulers, meanwhile, sneered at him and said, "He saved others, let him save himself if he is the chosen one, the Christ of God." Even the soldiers jeered at him. As they approached to offer him wine they called out, "If you are King of the Jews, save yourself." Above him there was an inscription that read, "This is the King of the Jews."

Now one of the criminals hanging there reviled Jesus, saying, "Are you not the Christ? Save yourself and us." The other, however, rebuking him, said in reply, "Have you no fear of God, for you are subject to the same condemnation? And indeed, we have been condemned justly, for the sentence we received corresponds to our crimes, but this man has done nothing criminal." Then he said, "Jesus, remember me when you come into your kingdom." He replied to him, "Amen, I say to you, today you will be with me in Paradise."

It was now about noon and darkness came over the whole land until three in the afternoon because of an eclipse of the sun. Then the veil of the temple was torn down the middle. Jesus cried out in a loud voice, "Father, into your hands I commend my spirit"; and when he had said this he breathed his last.

Here all kneel and pause for a short time.

The centurion who witnessed what had happened glorified God and said, "This man was innocent beyond doubt." When all the people who had gathered for this spectacle saw what had happened, they returned home beating their breasts; but all his acquaintances stood at a distance, including the women who had followed him from Galilee and saw these events.

Now there was a virtuous and righteous man named Joseph, who, though he was a member of the council, had not consented to their plan of action. He came from the Jewish town of Arimathea and was awaiting the kingdom of God. He went to Pilate and asked for the body of Jesus. After he had taken the body down, he wrapped it in a linen cloth and laid him in a rock-hewn tomb in which no one had yet been buried. It was the day of preparation, and the sabbath was about to begin. The women who had come from Galilee with him followed behind, and when they had seen the tomb and the way in which his body was laid in it, they returned and prepared spices and perfumed oils. Then they rested on the sabbath according to the commandment.

LUKE 22: 14-71 & 23: 1-56

Shorter form: LUKE 23:1-49

REFLECTION

Jesus appears in the Gospel of Luke as a model for all innocent people who suffer. Though he's forsaken by his disciples, his heavenly Father gives him support. In the garden, an angel comes to strengthen him. In turn, he strengthens others, continuing to remember in prayer those who accompany him. On Calvary, he reaches out mercifully to a thief and even to his enemies standing near his cross.

As disciples who waver and fall, we find Jesus in Luke's passion account urging us on and lifting our hearts with the promise of mercy he once made then: "This day you will be with me in Paradise."

Often enough, people mistake the sufferings of life or the inevitable valleys they pass through as signs of God's displeasure or unconcern. For St. Paul of the Cross these experiences become the time to trust fully in God's goodness. So he writes to a married man who feels he has lost all taste for spiritual things.

ST. PAUL OF THE CROSS

"Be thankful to God. You're not abandoned. God holds you like an infant against his breast. It may seem the fire of first fervor is gone, but God has hidden it under the ashes so that you may ground yourself in true humility and know your nothingness. A time will come when the Holy Spirit will blow upon the ashes, and a fire more lively and bright than before will be lit because you have been faithful to God" (Letter 1247, May 29, 1760).

PRAYER

Create in me a clean heart, O God,
and put a new and right spirit within me (Psalm 51).
Amen.

GOSPEL

Six days before Passover Jesus came to Bethany, where Lazarus was, whom Jesus had raised from the dead. They gave a dinner for him there, and Martha served, while Lazarus was one of those reclining at table with him. Mary took a liter of costly perfumed oil made from genuine aromatic nard and anointed the feet of Jesus and dried them with her hair; the house was filled with the fragrance of the oil. Then Judas the Iscariot, one of his disciples, and the one who would betray him, said, "Why was this oil not sold for three hundred days' wages and given to the poor?" He said this not because he cared about the poor but because he was a thief and held the money bag and used to steal the contributions. So Jesus said, "Leave her alone. Let her keep this for the day of my burial. You always have the poor with you, but you do not always have me."

The large crowd of the Jews found out that he was there and came, not only because of him, but also to see Lazarus, whom he had raised from the dead. And the chief priests plotted to kill Lazarus too, because many of the Jews were turning away and believing in Jesus because of him.

JOHN 12: 1-11

REFLECTION

John's Gospel calls us to a meal honoring Jesus in Bethany following the Resurrection of Lazarus. It's the last meal before the Passover supper. The gift of life that Jesus gives his friend leads to a sentence of death.

Faithful Martha serves the meal; Lazarus newly alive, is at the table. But the one drawing most of our attention is Mary, their sister who, sensing what's coming, kneels before Jesus to anoint his feet with precious oil and dry them with her hair. "And the house was filled with the fragrance of the oil."

The precious oil is an effusive sign of her love and gratitude; it also anoints Jesus for his burial. Only in passing does the Gospel mention that evil is in play here. Judas, "the one who would betray him," complains that the anointing is a waste, but his voice is silenced. Believers are honoring the one they love.

How fitting that Holy Week begins with this Gospel when, like Mary, we kneel and pour out the precious oil of our love upon him who pours out his precious life for us.

ST. PAUL OF THE CROSS

"May the holy cross of our good Jesus be ever planted in our hearts so that our souls may be grafted onto this tree of life and by the infinite merits of the death of the Author of life we may produce worthwhile fruits of penance" (Letter 11, August 29, 1726).

PRAYER

Let my prayer rise up before you like incense,
The raising of my hands like an evening offering (Psalm 141).
Amen.

GOSPEL

Reclining at table with his disciples, Jesus was deeply troubled and testified, "Amen, amen, I say to you, one of you will betray me." The disciples looked at one another, at a loss as to whom he meant. One of his disciples, the one whom Jesus loved, was reclining at Jesus' side. So Simon Peter nodded to him to find out whom he meant. He leaned back against Jesus' chest and said to him, "Master, who is it?" Jesus answered, "It is the one to whom I hand the morsel after I have dipped it." So he dipped the morsel and took it and handed it to Judas, son of Simon the Iscariot. After Judas took the morsel, Satan entered him. So Jesus said to him, "What you are going to do, do quickly." Now none of those reclining at table realized why he said this to him. Some thought that since Judas kept the money bag, Jesus had told him, "Buy what we need for the feast," or to give something to the poor. So Judas took the morsel and left at once. And it was night.

When he had left, Jesus said, "Now is the Son of Man glorified, and God is glorified in him. If God is glorified in him, God will also glorify him in himself, and he will glorify him at once. My children, I will be with you only a little while longer. You will look for me, and as I told the Jews, 'Where I go you cannot come,' so now I say it to you."

Simon Peter said to him, "Master, where are you going?" Jesus answered him, "Where I am going, you cannot follow me now, though you will follow later." Peter said to him, "Master, why can I not follow you now? I will lay down my life for you." Jesus answered, "Will you lay down your life for me? Amen, amen, I say to you, the cock will not crow before you deny me three times."

JOHN 13: 21-33, 36-38

REFLECTION

The Gospels for Monday to Thursday in Holy Week take us away from the crowded temple area in Jerusalem where Jesus spoke to the crowds and his avowed enemies and bring us into homes where "his own" join him to eat a meal. In Bethany six days before Passover he eats with those he loved: Martha, Mary, and Lazarus, whom he raised from the dead. In Jerusalem on the night before he dies he eats with the twelve who followed him.

During the meal in Bethany, Mary anoints his feet with precious oil in a beautiful outpouring of her love. But the Gospels for Tuesday and Wednesday point not to love but betrayal. Friends that followed him abandon him. Judas betrays him for thirty pieces of silver and goes out into the night; Peter will deny him three times; the others flee. Jesus must face suffering and death alone.

Are we unlike them?

Does a troubled Jesus face us too, "his own," to whom he gave new life in the waters of baptism and Bread at his table. Will we not betray or deny? Are we sure we will not go away? The Gospels are not just about long ago; they're also about now.

We think the saints exaggerate when they call themselves great sinners, but they know the truth. That's the way St. Paul of the Cross described himself in his account of his forty-day retreat as a young man.

ST. PAUL OF THE CROSS

"I rejoiced that our great God should wish to use so great a sinner, and on the other hand, I knew not where to cast myself, knowing myself so wretched. Enough! I know I shall tell my beloved Jesus that all creatures shall sing of his mercies" (Spiritual Diary, November 27, 1720).

PRAYER

Be my rock of refuge
a stronghold to give me safety.
For you are my rock and my fortress,
O God, rescue me from the hand of the wicked (Psalm 71).
Amen.

GOSPEL

One of the Twelve, who was called Judas Iscariot, went to the chief priests and said, "What are you willing to give me if I hand him over to you?" They paid him thirty pieces of silver, and from that time on he looked for an opportunity to hand him over.

On the first day of the Feast of Unleavened Bread, the disciples approached Jesus and said, "Where do you want us to prepare for you to eat the Passover?" He said, "Go into the city to a certain man and tell him, 'The teacher says, "My appointed time draws near; in your house I shall celebrate the Passover with my disciples."'" The disciples then did as Jesus had ordered, and prepared the Passover.

When it was evening, he reclined at table with the Twelve. And while they were eating, he said, "Amen, I say to you, one of you will betray me." Deeply distressed at this, they began to say to him one after another, "Surely it is not I, Lord?" He said in reply, "He who has dipped his hand into the dish with me is the one who will betray me. The Son of Man indeed goes, as it is written of him, but woe to that man by whom the Son of Man is betrayed. It would be better for that man if he had never been born." Then Judas, his betrayer, said in reply, "Surely it is not I, Rabbi?" He answered, "You have said so."

MATTHEW 26: 14-25

REFLECTION

The Gospels offer little information about the twelve disciples of Jesus. Peter is best known among them, since Jesus gave him a special role and also lived in his house in Capernaum.

Then, there's Judas. Matthew's Gospel gives more information about him than any other New Testament source and so it's read on "Spy Wednesday," the day in Holy Week that recalls Judas' offer to the rulers to hand Jesus over for thirty pieces of silver.

"Surely it is not I?" the disciples say one after the other when Jesus announces someone will betray him. And we say so too, as we watch Judas being pointed out. With Peter also we say we will not deny him. But the readings for these days caution us that there's a communion of sinners as well as a communion of saints. We're also sinful disciples. We are never far from the disciples who once sat at table with Jesus.

We come as sinners to the Easter Triduum, which begins the evening of Holy Thursday and ends on Easter Sunday. God shows great mercy; we hope for the forgiveness and new life that Jesus gave his disciples who left him the night before he died.

"We who wish to find the All, who is God, must cast ourselves into nothingness. God is "I AM"; we are they who are not, for dig as deeply as we can, we will find nothing, nothing. And we who are sinners are worse than nothing."

ST. PAUL OF THE CROSS

"God, out of nothing created the visible and invisible world. The infinite Good, by drawing good from evil through justifying sinners, performs a greater work of omnipotence than if he were to create a thousand worlds more vast and beautiful than this one. For in justifying sinners, he draws them from sin, an abyss darker and deeper than nothingness itself" (Letter 248, August 9, 1740).

PRAYER

"Lord, in your great love answer me" (Psalm 69).
Amen.

GOSPEL

Jesus came to Nazareth, where he had grown up, and went according to his custom into the synagogue on the sabbath day. He stood up to read and was handed a scroll of the prophet Isaiah. He unrolled the scroll and found the passage where it was written:

The Spirit of the Lord is upon me,
because he has anointed me
    to bring glad tidings to the poor.
He has sent me to proclaim liberty to captives
    and recovery of sight to the blind,
    to let the oppressed go free,
and to proclaim a year acceptable to the Lord.

Rolling up the scroll, he handed it back to the attendant and sat down, and the eyes of all in the synagogue looked intently at him. He said to them, "Today this Scripture passage is fulfilled in your hearing."

LUKE 4: 16-21

REFLECTION

"The Spirit of the Lord is upon me . . . He has anointed me," Jesus announces in the synagogue at Nazareth as he starts his public mission. Traditionally, for Jews an anointing with oil signified a conferral of grace, a gift of a mission, a selection of someone for a sacred role. In the synagogue, after reading from the Prophet Isaiah, Jesus says he has been anointed to follow in the footsteps of the prophets and to bring blessings to the world.

† The Chrism Mass is the annual Mass when the bishop blesses the oils that will be used for the sacraments throughout the year in the diocese.

His announcement, as we know, was not well received at Nazareth where he was seen as "the carpenter's son." But it did not matter—the Spirit of God had commissioned him.

At the Mass of Chrism celebrated today at the beginning of the Easter Triduum, the oils used by the church for its various sacraments are blessed and distributed—oil for catechumens, oil for the sick, oil for those to be confirmed or ordained. They bring blessings to the world. At the same time, those principally charged with bestowing these holy signs—bishops and priests—are reminded of the holy task that's theirs as ministers of the church.

Like bread and wine, oil is so common and ordinary; we may think it's nothing. But once blessed, it becomes holy and brings blessings. It signifies the Spirit of God is present and at work. If oil can be holy, then we can be too. Blessing oil as we celebrate the mystery of the Resurrection is a sign that our world becomes holy through Jesus, our Lord.

St. Paul of the Cross, like so many other saints, often said he was a sinner. His biographer, St. Vincent Strambi wrote:

"People were puzzled by his frequent assertion that he was a great sinner. 'I leave nothing to this congregation but the stench of my vices and bad example.' Sometimes he said it facetiously. On the feast of St. Anthony of the Desert, when they blessed the animals of the retreat, he told the rector of Terracina: "When you bless them, get Brother Bartholomew to throw some ribbons on me and bless me too. I'm one of them."

ST. PAUL OF THE CROSS

"Yet in a letter he writes, 'Certainly I am dear to God, and why? Because I'm the wretch that I am. Jesus came not to call the just but sinners. How dear we sinners are to him'" (Life of Paul of the Cross, chapter 3).

PRAYER

Lord, bless our earth, our sea and sky,
and make them holy.
Bless our fields and mountains, rivers and streams,
and make them holy.
We who live and breathe
praise you, O Lord.
Amen.

PASCHAL
TRIDUUM

GOSPEL

Before the feast of Passover, Jesus knew that his hour had come to pass from this world to the Father. He loved his own in the world and he loved them to the end. The devil had already induced Judas, son of Simon the Iscariot, to hand him over. So, during supper, fully aware that the Father had put everything into his power and that he had come from God and was returning to God, he rose from supper and took off his outer garments. He took a towel and tied it around his waist. Then he poured water into a basin and began to wash the disciples' feet and dry them with the towel around his waist. He came to Simon Peter, who said to him, "Master, are you going to wash my feet?" Jesus answered and said to him, "What I am doing, you do not understand now, but you will understand later." Peter said to him, "You will never wash my feet." Jesus answered him, "Unless I wash you, you will have no inheritance with me." Simon Peter said to him, "Master, then not only my feet, but my hands and head as well." Jesus said to him, "Whoever has bathed has no need except to have his feet washed, for he is clean all over; so you are clean, but not all." For he knew who would betray him; for this reason, he said, "Not all of you are clean."

So when he had washed their feet and put his garments back on and reclined at table again, he said to them, "Do you realize what I have done for you? You call me 'teacher' and 'master,' and rightly so, for indeed I am. If I, therefore, the master and teacher, have washed your feet, you ought to wash one another's feet. I have given you a model to follow, so that as I have done for you, you should also do."

JOHN 13: 1-15

REFLECTION

"Love makes one little room an everywhere." That was so when Jesus entered the supper room in Jerusalem to eat with his disciples on the night before he died. A dark fate awaited him as powerful forces readied to take his life. His disciples, "his own who were in the world," were arguing among themselves as they took their places at table.

What would he do? Understandably he might respond with disappointment, like the servant whom the prophet Isaiah described, "I toiled in vain; and for nothing, uselessly, spent my strength" (Is 49).

Jesus, however, took bread and gave it to his disciples. "Take this," he said, "this is my body." He took the cup and gave it to them. "This is my blood, the blood of the new covenant, to be poured out in behalf of many."

That night, without wariness or regret, he gave himself to his Father and to his disciples. As our Savior and Redeemer he gave himself unhesitatingly for the life of the world. In the supper room a love was tested and a love was displayed that reached everywhere.

ST. PAUL OF THE CROSS

Evening of Holy Thursday.

"Now is not the time to write, rather to weep. Jesus is dead to give us life. All creatures are mourning, the sun is darkened, the earth quakes, the rocks are rent, the veil of the temple is torn. Only my heart remains harder than flint. I will say no more. Join the poor mother of the dead Jesus as her companion. Ask the dear Magdalene and John where their hearts are. Let the sea of their pains flood within you. I end at the foot of the cross" (Letter 181, April 3, 1738).

PRAYER

How shall I make a return to the Lord
for the goodness he has shown to me?
The cup of salvation I will take up
and call on the name of the Lord (Psalm 116).
Amen.

GOSPEL

Jesus went out with his disciples across the Kidron valley to where there was a garden, into which he and his disciples entered. Judas his betrayer also knew the place, because Jesus had often met there with his disciples. So Judas got a band of soldiers and guards from the chief priests and the Pharisees and went there with lanterns, torches, and weapons. Jesus, knowing everything that was going to happen to him, went out and said to them, "Whom are you looking for?" They answered him, "Jesus the Nazorean." He said to them, "I AM." Judas his betrayer was also with them. When he said to them, "I AM," they turned away and fell to the ground. So he again asked them, "Whom are you looking for?" They said, "Jesus the Nazorean." Jesus answered, "I told you that I AM. So if you are looking for me, let these men go." This was to fulfill what he had said, "I have not lost any of those you gave me." Then Simon Peter, who had a sword, drew it, struck the high priest's slave, and cut off his right ear. The slave's name was Malchus. Jesus said to Peter, "Put your sword into its scabbard. Shall I not drink the cup that the Father gave me?"

So the band of soldiers, the tribune, and the Jewish guards seized Jesus, bound him, and brought him to Annas first. He was the father-in-law of Caiaphas, who was high priest that year. It was Caiaphas who had counseled the Jews that it was better that one man should die rather than the people.

Simon Peter and another disciple followed Jesus. Now the other disciple was known to the high priest, and he entered the courtyard of the high priest with Jesus. But Peter stood at the gate outside. So the other disciple, the acquaintance of the high priest, went out and spoke to the gatekeeper and brought Peter in. Then the maid who was the gatekeeper said to Peter, "You are not one of this man's disciples, are you?" He said, "I am not." Now the slaves and the guards were standing around a charcoal fire that they had made, because it was cold, and were warming themselves. Peter was also standing there keeping warm.

The high priest questioned Jesus about his disciples and about his doctrine. Jesus answered him, "I have spoken publicly to the world. I have always taught in a synagogue or in the temple area where all the Jews gather, and in secret I have said nothing. Why ask me? Ask those who heard me what I said to them. They know what I said." When he had said this, one of the temple guards standing there struck Jesus and said, "Is this the way you answer the high priest?" Jesus answered him, "If I have spoken wrongly, testify to the wrong; but if I have spoken rightly, why do you strike me?" Then Annas sent him bound to Caiaphas the high priest.

Now Simon Peter was standing there keeping warm. And they said to him, "You are not one of his disciples, are you?" He denied it and said, "I am not." One of the slaves of the high priest, a relative of the one whose ear Peter had cut off, said, "Didn't I see you in the garden with him?" Again Peter denied it. And immediately the cock crowed.

Then they brought Jesus from Caiaphas to the praetorium. It was morning. And they themselves did not enter the praetorium, in order not to be defiled so that they could eat the Passover. So Pilate came out to them and said, "What charge do you bring against this man?" They answered and said to him, "If he were not a criminal, we would not have handed him over to you." At this, Pilate said to them, "Take him yourselves, and judge him according to your law." The Jews answered him, "We do not have the right to execute anyone," in order that the word of Jesus might be fulfilled that he said indicating the kind of death he would die. So Pilate went back into the praetorium and summoned Jesus and said to him, "Are you the King of the Jews?" Jesus answered, "Do you say this on your own or have others told you about me?" Pilate answered, "I am not a Jew, am I? Your own nation and the chief priests handed you over to me. What have you done?" Jesus answered, "My kingdom does not belong to this world. If my kingdom did belong to this world, my attendants would be fighting to keep me from being handed over to the Jews. But as it is, my kingdom is not here." So Pilate said to him, "Then you are a king?" Jesus answered, "You say I am a king. For this I was born and for this I came into the world, to testify to the truth. Everyone who belongs to the truth listens to my voice." Pilate said to him, "What is truth?"

When he had said this, he again went out to the Jews and said to them, "I find no guilt in him. But you have a custom that I release one prisoner to you at Passover. Do you want me to release to you the King of the Jews?" They cried out again, "Not this one but Barabbas!" Now Barabbas was a revolutionary.

Then Pilate took Jesus and had him scourged. And the soldiers wove a crown out of thorns and placed it on his head, and clothed him in a purple cloak, and they came to him and said, "Hail, King of the Jews!" And they struck him repeatedly. Once more Pilate went out and said to them, "Look, I am bringing him out to you, so that you may know that I find no guilt in him." So Jesus came out, wearing the crown of thorns and the purple cloak. And he said to them, "Behold, the man!" When the chief priests and the guards saw him they cried out, "Crucify him, crucify him!" Pilate said to them, "Take him yourselves and crucify him. I find no guilt in him." The Jews answered, "We have a law, and according to that law he ought to die, because he made himself the Son of God." Now when Pilate heard this statement, he became even more afraid, and went back into the praetorium and said to Jesus, "Where are you from?" Jesus did not answer him. So Pilate said to him, "Do you not speak to me? Do you not know that I have power to release you and I have power to crucify you?" Jesus answered him, "You would have no power over me if it had not been given to you from above. For this reason the one who handed me over to you has the greater sin." Consequently, Pilate tried to release him; but the Jews cried out, "If you release him, you are not a Friend of

Caesar. Everyone who makes himself a king opposes Caesar."

When Pilate heard these words he brought Jesus out and seated him on the judge's bench in the place called Stone Pavement, in Hebrew, Gabbatha. It was preparation day for Passover, and it was about noon. And he said to the Jews, "Behold, your king!" They cried out, "Take him away, take him away! Crucify him!" Pilate said to them, "Shall I crucify your king?" The chief priests answered, "We have no king but Caesar." Then he handed him over to them to be crucified.

So they took Jesus, and, carrying the cross himself, he went out to what is called the Place of the Skull, in Hebrew, Golgotha. There they crucified him, and with him two others, one on either side, with Jesus in the middle. Pilate also had an inscription written and put on the cross. It read, "Jesus the Nazorean, the King of the Jews." Now many of the Jews read this inscription, because the place where Jesus was crucified was near the city; and it was written in Hebrew, Latin, and Greek. So the chief priests of the Jews said to Pilate, "Do not write 'The King of the Jews,' but that he said, 'I am the King of the Jews'." Pilate answered, "What I have written, I have written."

When the soldiers had crucified Jesus, they took his clothes and divided them into four shares, a share for each soldier. They also took his tunic, but the tunic was seamless, woven in one piece from the top down. So they said to one another, "Let's not tear it, but cast lots for it to see whose it will be," in order that the passage of Scripture might be fulfilled that says:

They divided my garments among them,
and for my vesture they cast lots.

This is what the soldiers did. Standing by the cross of Jesus were his mother and his mother's sister, Mary the wife of Clopas, and Mary of Magdala. When Jesus saw his mother and the disciple there whom he loved he said to his mother, "Woman, behold, your son." Then he said to the disciple, "Behold, your mother." And from that hour the disciple took her into his home.

After this, aware that everything was now finished, in order that the Scripture might be fulfilled, Jesus said, "I thirst." There was a vessel filled with common wine. So they put a sponge soaked in wine on a sprig of hyssop and put it up to his mouth. When Jesus had taken the wine, he said, "It is finished." And bowing his head, he handed over the spirit.

Here all kneel and pause for a short time.

Now since it was preparation day, in order that the bodies might not remain on the cross on the sabbath, for the sabbath day of that week was a solemn one, the Jews asked Pilate that their legs be broken and that they be taken down. So the soldiers came and broke the legs of the first and then of the other one who was crucified with Jesus. But when they came to Jesus and saw that he was already dead, they did not break his legs, but one soldier thrust his lance into his side, and immediately blood and water flowed out. An eyewitness has testified, and his testimony is true; he knows that he is speaking the truth, so that you also may come to believe. For this happened so that the Scripture passage might be fulfilled: *Not a bone of it will be broken.* And again another passage says: *They will look upon him whom they have pierced.*

After this, Joseph of Arimathea, secretly a disciple of Jesus for fear of the Jews, asked Pilate if he could remove the body of Jesus. And Pilate permitted it. So he came and took his body. Nicodemus, the one who had first come to him at night, also came bringing a mixture of myrrh and aloes weighing about one hundred pounds. They took the body of Jesus and bound it with burial cloths along with the spices, according to the Jewish burial custom. Now in the place where he had been crucified there was a garden, and in the garden a new tomb, in which no one had yet been buried. So they laid Jesus there because of the Jewish preparation day; for the tomb was close by.

JOHN 18: 1-40 & 19: 1-42

REFLECTION

We solemnly celebrate the death and Resurrection of our Lord on Holy Thursday, Good Friday, and Holy Saturday, using the simplest of signs. On Holy Thursday Jesus knelt before his disciples and washed their feet. At table he gave them in bread and wine his own body and blood as signs of his love for them and for all humanity.

On Good Friday we take another symbol, the cross, a powerful sign of death, which first struck fear into the hearts of Jesus' disciples, but then as they recalled the Lord's journey from the garden to Calvary, as they saw the empty tomb, as they were taught by the Risen Jesus himself, they began to see that God can conquer even death itself.

On this day, we read the memories of John, the Lord's disciple, who followed him from the Sea of Galilee, to Jerusalem, its temple and its feasts, to Calvary where he stood with the women and watched the Lord die. Like the others, he recoiled before it all, but then saw signs of victory even in the garden, in the judgment hall, before Pilate, and finally in the cross itself.

On this darkest of days, Christ's victory is proclaimed in John's Gospel.

ST. PAUL OF THE CROSS

Go into my opened side,
Opened by the spear,
Go within and there abide
For my love is here (Letter 251, September 5, 1740).

PRAYER

We adore you, O Christ, and we bless you.
By your cross you have redeemed the world.
Amen.

GOSPEL

After the sabbath, as the first day of the week was dawning, Mary Magdalene and the other Mary came to see the tomb. And behold, there was a great earthquake; for an angel of the Lord descended from heaven, approached, rolled back the stone, and sat upon it. His appearance was like lightning and his clothing was white as snow. The guards were shaken with fear of him and became like dead men. Then the angel said to the women in reply, "Do not be afraid! I know that you are seeking Jesus the crucified. He is not here, for he has been raised just as he said. Come and see the place where he lay. Then go quickly and tell his disciples, 'He has been raised from the dead, and he is going before you to Galilee; there you will see him.' Behold, I have told you." Then they went away quickly from the tomb, fearful yet overjoyed, and ran to announce this to his disciples. And behold, Jesus met them on their way and greeted them. They approached, embraced his feet, and did him homage. Then Jesus said to them, "Do not be afraid. Go tell my brothers to go to Galilee, and there they will see me."

MATTHEW 28: 1-10

REFLECTION

We have to let each of the evangelists tell us the story of Jesus' Resurrection in their own way. It's "after the Sabbath as the first day of the week was dawning," when Jesus rises from the tomb, according to Matthew. His Resurrection ushers in a new day, a new age that changes the world itself. The earthquakes announcing the momentous event; an angel appears to roll back the heavy stone that seals his grave, announcing the wondrous mystery.

Two humble witnesses, two women, are the first to know. Come to keep a lonely watch at his grave, Mary Magdalene and the other Mary are like the shepherds at his birth to whom an angel tells the good news: "Do not be afraid, I know you are seeking Jesus the crucified. He is not here, for he has been raised, just as he said."

They're told to look into the empty tomb and then without delay go tell his disciples to return to Galilee where they will see him.

On their way, running quickly, "fearful yet overjoyed" Jesus meets them. "They embraced his feet and did him homage."

Matthew's account ends as Jesus sends his disciples into the whole world from a mountain in Galilee to announce the good news, "making disciples of all nations, baptizing them in the name of the Father, and of the Son, and of the Holy Spirit, and teaching them to obey everything that I have commanded you. And remember: I am with you always, to the end of the age."

It's a fast-breaking story; the whole world must quickly know about it. There can be no delay. It's urgent to get the news out.

Saints of every age experience this same urgency about the Gospel. The Resurrection of Jesus is not a mystery they weigh or slowly consider. It must be told "in season and out of season."

Saints like St. Paul of the Cross have a tireless zeal. In his eighties, deaf and crippled by sicknesses, Paul was asked by Pope Clement XIV to preach a mission in the square before the church of Santa Maria in Trastevere in Rome. He accepted the invitation and with the zeal that marked him as a young man he preached to the crowds that flocked to hear him.

ST. PAUL OF THE CROSS

Paul, the venerable servant of God, thinking himself incapable of preaching any more, had given up preaching missions some years before an extraordinary church jubilee was declared by the pope in 1769. The pope wanted a mission preached to the people of Rome and appointed Cardinal Colonna to name the missionaries. He immediately called Father Paul.

The old priest excused himself, saying that his strength had failed, he was almost an invalid, and he was also deaf. The good cardinal smiled and replied, "Your voice is good enough and as for your hearing, it's more important that your hearers aren't deaf."

Though he was weak and the weather was hot, Father Paul prepared for the mission that was to take place in the piazza before the Church of St. Mary in Trastevere.

Despite a weak-spell beforehand, he climbed unto the platform to announce the truths of faith to the Roman people. An unusual crowd assembled to hear the man of God: people of all ranks and conditions gathered. The fruit produced by his sermons was marvelous. The vast crowd was hushed into breathless silence and melted into tears of contrition by the voice of the feeble old man. The sight of his venerable form, with uncovered head and sandelled feet, hardly able to stand upright, and tottering up the platform steps with the help of several assistants, was enough to win the inmost hearts of all who saw him and produced the most unheard of effects on their souls.

His sermon no sooner ended than people crowded around him to kiss his hand and touch his habit. By the last day of the mission, the crowd was so great that the cardinal in charge of the church had to station soldiers to keep order. Father Paul's last sermon was crowned with success. But the old man, wary of the applause, went home as soon as he could.

(Life of Paul of the Cross, by St. Vincent Strambi, chapter 38)

PRAYER

Lord,
let me look into the empty tomb
and know the surprise and joy of the women
who came seeking Jesus crucified.
Give me their zeal to make you known
to all the world.
Give me a faith that will never leave me.
Amen.

GOSPEL

When the sabbath was over, Mary Magdalene, Mary, the mother of James, and Salome bought spices so that they might go and anoint him. Very early when the sun had risen, on the first day of the week, they came to the tomb. They were saying to one another, "Who will roll back the stone for us from the entrance to the tomb?" When they looked up, they saw that the stone had been rolled back; it was very large. On entering the tomb they saw a young man sitting on the right side, clothed in a white robe, and they were utterly amazed. He said to them, "Do not be amazed! You seek Jesus of Nazareth, the crucified. He has been raised; he is not here. Behold the place where they laid him. "But go and tell his disciples and Peter, 'He is going before you to Galilee; there you will see him, as he told you.'"

MARK 16: 1-7

REFLECTION

Mark's Gospel of the Resurrection of Jesus begins with Mary Magdalene, Mary the mother of James, and Salome. They are among the many women who came up to Jerusalem with Jesus from Galilee. They had provided for him in his ministry; they had looked on from a distance when he was crucified; now they provide for him in his death (Mk 15:40–41).

Early Sunday morning, the sun now up, the three women come to finish anointing his body, only hastily done on Good Friday.

Part of the hard task they see before them was the removal of the huge stone blocking access to his tomb. How would they roll it away? They're surprised to find it rolled away, the tomb empty, and a young man dressed in a white robe telling them not to be afraid. Jesus has been raised. They are to go and tell his other disciples that he will meet them in Galilee where they will see him.

"So they went out and fled from the tomb, for terror and amazement had seized them, and they said nothing to anyone, for they were afraid" (Mk 16:8).

The frightened women flee from the tomb, Mark's Gospel says. His Gospel insists on our human tendency to unbelief and it sees it even here at the empty tomb. The women remind us that the Resurrection of Jesus is not an easily accepted mystery. To believe demands an experience of suffering. The stone has to be rolled away, and only God can do that for us.

Sharing the cross of Jesus leads to belief in his Resurrection. That was the teaching of St. Paul of the Cross.

ST. PAUL OF THE CROSS

"Without a doubt, you will gain the victory; in paradise you will sing a hymn as you gain the strength of your Savior. . . . What peace is prepared for you after the battle. What a crown the Supreme Good wishes to bestow on you. Jesus and Mary are waiting for you, they will dry your tears" (Letter 39, January 3, 1729).

PRAYER

O God,
take me to the tomb with the holy women.
Take the stone away that I may see.
Amen.

GOSPEL

At daybreak on the first day of the week the women who had come from Galilee with Jesus took the spices they had prepared and went to the tomb. They found the stone rolled away from the tomb; but when they entered, they did not find the body of the Lord Jesus. While they were puzzling over this, behold, two men in dazzling garments appeared to them. They were terrified and bowed their faces to the ground. They said to them, "Why do you seek the living one among the dead? He is not here, but he has been raised. Remember what he said to you while he was still in Galilee, that the Son of Man must be handed over to sinners and be crucified, and rise on the third day." And they remembered his words. Then they returned from the tomb and announced all these things to the eleven and to all others. The women were Mary Magdalene, Joanna, and Mary the mother of James; the others who accompanied them also told this to the apostles, but their story seemed like nonsense and they did not believe them. But Peter got up and ran to the tomb, bent down, and saw the burial cloths alone; then he went home amazed at what had happened.

LUKE 24: 1-12

REFLECTION

According to Luke's account of the Resurrection, some of the women from Galilee who provided for Jesus and accompanied him to Jerusalem went to his tomb early at dawn. They had seen Joseph Arimathea take the body of Jesus after his death, wrap it in a linen cloth and carry it there. Buying spices, they went to anoint the body as customary.

They find an empty tomb and are puzzled. Suddenly, "two men in dazzling clothes" stand before them and the women are awestruck. The two are witnesses. "Why do you look for the living among the dead?" they're asked. The women are reminded of Jesus' predictions that he would rise on the third day after suffering, and they return to tell the eleven disciples and the rest.

Their message isn't believed at first.

Luke's Gospel tells of similar unbelief in the two disciples on their way to Emmaus. But gradually as Jesus appears to one and the others, they recognize him. He has risen as he said.

Luke's Gospel, in the story of Emmaus, will stress the scriptures and "the breaking of the bread" as our means to belief. These great signs still bring us into the presence of the Risen Christ.

It was faith in the Risen Christ that inspired the words spoken so often by St. Paul of the Cross to those burdened by sorrow:

ST. PAUL OF THE CROSS

"Live then with your heart raised up in God and do not allow yourself to be crushed by sadness, and be sure that one day you will see the warm sun that will scatter these clouds" (Letter 273, May 15, 1741).

PRAYER

Lord Jesus Christ,
stay with us as we go on our way.
Open our eyes and lift up our hearts
with your inspired words and signs.
May we know you in "the breaking of the bread,"
light the fire of faith within us.
Amen.

EASTER
SUNDAY

GOSPEL

On the first day of the week, Mary of Magdala came to the tomb early in the morning, while it was still dark, and saw the stone removed from the tomb. So she ran and went to Simon Peter and to the other disciple whom Jesus loved, and told them, "They have taken the Lord from the tomb, and we don't know where they put him." So Peter and the other disciple went out and came to the tomb. They both ran, but the other disciple ran faster than Peter and arrived at the tomb first; he bent down and saw the burial cloths there, but did not go in. When Simon Peter arrived after him, he went into the tomb and saw the burial cloths there, and the cloth that had covered his head, not with the burial cloths but rolled up in a separate place. Then the other disciple also went in, the one who had arrived at the tomb first, and he saw and believed. For they did not yet understand the Scripture that he had to rise from the dead.

JOHN 20: 1-9

Alternative readings from Easter Vigil or LUKE 24:13-35 at an afternoon or evening Mass.

REFLECTION

Beside Peter, Mary Magdalene is a key witness to the Resurrection of Jesus. Her story is told in John's Gospel which speaks of their meeting in the garden. For the rest of her years Mary would remember those moments by the tomb.

In the morning darkness she came weeping for the one she thought lost forever. She heard him call her name, "Mary". She turned to see him alive and the garden became paradise.

Like a new Eve she was sent by Jesus to bring news of life to all the living. She was his apostle to the apostles. The belief of Christians in the Resurrection of Jesus rests in part on this woman's word. Today the church questions her:

Tell us, Mary, what did you see on the way?

"I saw the tomb of the now living Christ.

I saw the glory of Christ, now risen.

I saw angels who gave witness;

the cloths, too, which once covered head and limbs.

Christ my hope had indeed arisen.

He will go before his own into Galilee."

The Easter mystery brightens the vision of Christians ever since. Here Paul of the Cross reflects on its wonder.

ST. PAUL OF THE CROSS

"O True God, what will our hearts be like when we swim in that infinite sea of sweetness! What will it be like when we are all transformed by love in God, and we will be happy with that infinite goodness with which our God is happy! We will sing in eternity the divine mercies, the triumphs of the Immaculate Lamb and of Mary, our most holy Mother! What will it be when we sing "Holy, Holy, Holy," and when with all the saints we sing Alleluia! When we are united to God more than iron is united to fire, for without ceasing to be iron, it seems all fire, so we are transformed into God that the soul will be completely divinized. Oh, when will that day come! When, when will death come to break the wall of this prison!" (Letter 162, August 29, 1737).

PRAYER

Give thanks to the Lord for he is good,

for his mercy endures forever.

The stone that the builders rejected

has become the cornerstone.

By the Lord has this been done,

it is wonderful in our eyes (Psalm 118).

Amen.

EPILOGUE

I know I shouldn't do it, but I will. What would St. Paul of the Cross say if he were with us today? Is it a futile question to ask? So much has changed since he toiled long and hard in the Tuscan Maremma, the poorest area in poor Italy in the eighteenth century. Now it's a trendy tourist destination since its swamplands were finally filled in the last seventy years.

The world has changed too. A pope is still in Rome, but the Church is so much bigger and worldwide than before. Through instant communications and trade the world's grown closer. Its peoples mix constantly in the global marketplace. Its disasters, crop failures, wars, and emerging economies are speedily shared.

I don't think our saint would be out of place today, though. He had zeal, and zeal moves us to be where we must be. He had faith and loved the message of Jesus Christ; he would find the way to live that faith himself and bring it to others.

Our times could use his spirituality. We need to pray more deeply and go before the mystery of God and rest in the Divine Presence. There, more than anywhere, we learn how to live and move and be. As Paul said long ago, "The world is sliding into a profound forgetfulness of the bitter suffering endured out of love by Jesus Christ, our true Good." Prayer is a remedy for forgetfulness.

Paul was a "Hunter of Souls." He wasn't afraid to walk on risky roads into unknown towns to bring the Gospel to the poor. We need a church today willing to hunt for the lost and bring them safely home.

I think he would like our time. It's challenging, like the world of his day.

APPENDIX A:
CALENDAR OF LENT 2011–2020
& LECTIONARY CYCLE

Ash Wednesday–Easter

Year	Sunday Year	Lent	Date
2011	A	Ash Wednesday	March 9
		1st Sunday of Lent	March 13
		2nd Sunday of Lent	March 20
		3rd Sunday of Lent	March 27
		4th Sunday of Lent	April 3
		5th Sunday of Lent	April 10
		Palm Sunday	April 17
		Paschal Triduum	April 21
		Easter Sunday	April 24
2012	B	Ash Wednesday	February 22
		1st Sunday of Lent	February 26
		2nd Sunday of Lent	March 4
		3rd Sunday of Lent	March 11
		4th Sunday of Lent	March 18
		5th Sunday of Lent	March 25
		Palm Sunday	April 1
		Paschal Triduum	April 5
		Easter Sunday	April 8

Year	Sunday Year	Lent	Date
2013	C	Ash Wednesday	February 13
		1st Sunday of Lent	February 17
		2nd Sunday of Lent	February 24
		3rd Sunday of Lent	March 3
		4th Sunday of Lent	March 10
		5th Sunday of Lent	March 17
		Palm Sunday	March 24
		Paschal Triduum	March 28
		Easter Sunday	March 31
2014	A	Ash Wednesday	March 5
		1st Sunday of Lent	March 9
		2nd Sunday of Lent	March 16
		3rd Sunday of Lent	March 23
		4th Sunday of Lent	March 30
		5th Sunday of Lent	April 6
		Palm Sunday	April 13
		Paschal Triduum	April 17
		Easter Sunday	April 20

Year	Sunday Year	Lent	Date
2015	B	Ash Wednesday	February 18
		1st Sunday of Lent	February 22
		2nd Sunday of Lent	March 1
		3rd Sunday of Lent	March 8
		4th Sunday of Lent	March 15
		5th Sunday of Lent	March 22
		Palm Sunday	March 29
		Paschal Triduum	April 2
		Easter Sunday	April 5
2016	C	Ash Wednesday	February 10
		1st Sunday of Lent	February 14
		2nd Sunday of Lent	February 21
		3rd Sunday of Lent	February 28
		4th Sunday of Lent	March 6
		5th Sunday of Lent	March 13
		Palm Sunday	March 20
		Paschal Triduum	March 24
		Easter Sunday	March 27

Year	Sunday Year	Lent	Date
2017	A	Ash Wednesday	March 1
		1st Sunday of Lent	March 5
		2nd Sunday of Lent	March 12
		3rd Sunday of Lent	March 19
		4th Sunday of Lent	March 26
		5th Sunday of Lent	April 2
		Palm Sunday	April 9
		Paschal Triduum	April 13
		Easter Sunday	April 16
2018	B	Ash Wednesday	February 14
		1st Sunday of Lent	February 18
		2nd Sunday of Lent	February 25
		3rd Sunday of Lent	March 4
		4th Sunday of Lent	March 11
		5th Sunday of Lent	March 18
		Palm Sunday	March 25
		Paschal Triduum	March 29
		Easter Sunday	April 1

Year	Sunday Year	Lent	Date
2019	C	Ash Wednesday	March 6
		1st Sunday of Lent	March 10
		2nd Sunday of Lent	March 17
		3rd Sunday of Lent	March 24
		4th Sunday of Lent	March 31
		5th Sunday of Lent	April 7
		Palm Sunday	April 14
		Paschal Triduum	April 18
		Easter Sunday	April 21
2020	A	Ash Wednesday	February 26
		1st Sunday of Lent	March 1
		2nd Sunday of Lent	March 8
		3rd Sunday of Lent	March 15
		4th Sunday of Lent	March 22
		5th Sunday of Lent	March 29
		Palm Sunday	April 5
		Paschal Triduum	April 9
		Easter Sunday	April 12

APPENDIX B:
SELECTIONS FROM THE WRITINGS OF ST. PAUL OF THE CROSS

Ash Wednesday	Letter 1766, December 29, 1768
Thursday	Letter 1135, June 8, 1758
Friday	Diary, January 1, 1721
Saturday	Diary, November 27, 1720
1st Sunday A	Diary, December 10–13, 1720
1st Sunday B	Diary, November 23, 1720
1st Sunday C	Diary, November 25, 1720
Monday 1	Letter 12, February 21, 1722
Tuesday 1	Letter 752, May 25, 1751
Wednesday 1	Letter 1033, July 20, 1756
Thursday 1	Letter 920, September 3, 1754
Friday 1	Letter 525, March 16, 1748
Saturday 1	Letter 1156, August 31, 1758
2nd Sunday A	Letter 1194, May 26, 1759
2nd Sunday B	Letter 752, May 25, 1751
2nd Sunday C	Letter 764, July 20, 1751
Monday 2	Letter 67, December 14, 1733
Tuesday 2	Letter 863, August 14, 1753
Wednesday 2	Letter 12, February 21, 1722
Thursday 2	Letter 27, September 3, 1735
Friday 2	Letter 132, January 24, 1737
Saturday 2	Letter 26, December 23, 1734
3rd Sunday A	Letter 662, August 9, 1749
3rd Sunday B	Letter 1765, December 28, 1768
3rd Sunday C	Letter 937, January 28, 1755

Monday 3	Letter 47, November 29, 1730
Tuesday 3	Life of Blessed Paul of the Cross, Chapter 32
Wednesday 3	Letter 1114, March 1, 1758
Thursday 3	Letter 1188, March 29, 1759
Friday 3	Letter 23, March 17, 1734
Saturday 3	Letter 1033, July 20, 1756
4th Sunday A	Letter 929, December 21, 1754
4th Sunday B	Letter 920, September 3, 1754
4th Sunday C	Life of Blessed Paul of the Cross, Chapter 11
Monday 4	Letter 914, July 23, 1754
Tuesday 4	Letter 41, September 7, 1729
Wednesday 4	Letter 1464, May 26, 1764
Thursday 4	Life of Blessed Paul of the Cross, Chapter 35
Friday 4	Letter 1033, July 20, 1756
Saturday 4	Letter 1180, February 1, 1759
5th Sunday A	Letter 1925, November 26, 1770
5th Sunday B	Letter 266, January 10, 1741
5th Sunday C	Diary, December 28, 1720
Monday 5 Years A and B	Life of Blessed Paul of the Cross, Chapter 14
Monday Year C	Letter 11, August 29, 1726
Tuesday 5	Letter 266, January 10, 1741
Wednesday 5	Letter 18, December 30, 1730
Thursday 5	Letter 18, December 30, 1730

SUGGESTIONS FOR FURTHER READING

PRIMARY SOURCES

St. Paul of the Cross. *Words from the Heart: A Selection from the Personal Letters of St. Paul of the Cross.* Translated and annotated by Edmund Burke, C.P., Roger Mercurio, C.P., and Silvan Rouse, C.P. Dublin, 1976.

_____. *Letters of Saint Paul of the Cross.* 3 vols. Translated by Roger Mercurio, C.P. and Frederick Sucher, C.P. Edited by Laurence Finn, C.P. and Donald Webber, C.P. Hyde Park, NY, 2000. Translations herein revised by the author.

BIOGRAPHIES AND STUDIES OF ST. PAUL OF THE CROSS

Bennett, Kelley, C.P. *Listen to his Love: The Life of St. Paul of the Cross.* Union City, NJ, 1984. Also available in DVD (2005).

_____. *Living Wisdom for Everyday.* Catholic Book Company: Totowa, NJ, 1994.

_____. *Spiritual Direction According to St. Paul of the Cross.* Union City, NJ, 2007.

Bialas, Martin, C.P. *The Mysticism of the Passion in St. Paul of the Cross.* San Francisco, 1990.

Cingolani, Gabriele. *St. Paul of the Cross.* Union City, NJ, 1994.

Mead, Jude, C.P. *St. Paul of the Cross: A Source/Workbook.* New Rochelle, NY, 1983.

Spencer, Paul Francis, C.P. *As a Seal Upon Your Heart.* Kildare, Ireland, 1994.

Strambi, Vincent. *Blessed Paul of the Cross.* London, 1853.

INTERNET
RESOURCES

Passionist Congregation: International Web site available at:
http://www.passiochristi.org/eN/eN.htm

Passionists USA: Eastern Province Web site available at:
www.thepassionists.org

Passionists USA: Western Province Web site available at:
http://www.passionist.org

Passionists International Web site available at:
http://www.passionistsinternational.org

Passionist Nuns Web site available at:
http://www.passionistnuns.org

Passionist Sisters of the Cross and Passion Web site available at:
http://www.passionistsisters.org/Home.html

Passionist Media Web site available at:
http://crossplace.com

http://thesundaymass.org

http://vimeo.com/user1344343/videos/sort:date

http://thepassionists.org/reflections/

Passionist Archives Web site available at:
http://www.cpprovince.org/archives/

The Passionist Charism Web site available at:
http://passionistcharism.wordpress.com

Bread on the Waters: Words of St. Paul of the Cross Web site available at:
www.cptryon.org

Christus Publishing, LLC Web site available at:
http://www.christuspublishing.com

COVER ART

The detail of the painting, "St. Paul of the Cross" by an unknown artist.

ABOUT THE
AUTHOR

Father Victor Hoagland, C.P, preaches at parish missions and retreats for priests, religious, and laity throughout the United States and is the director of Passionist Press, which publishes material pertaining to the Passionists and their ministry.

A member of the U.S. Passionists' eastern province, he studied at the Catholic University of America and the Gregorian University in Rome. Afterwards, he taught liturgy, sacramental theology, and spirituality to seminarians of his own community and at St. John's University, Queens, New York. He also served in the provincial administration of his province.

Among his writings are *The Book of Saints, Saints of the New Testament, Mary the Mother of God, Daily Prayers* (Regina Press) and *Following Jesus Christ* (Passionist Press).

Fr. Victor is principal contributor to *Bread on the Waters,* (www.cptryon.org), a popular website on Catholic spirituality that contains a wealth of religious materials for young children and instructions on prayer. He blogs at Victor's Place (http://vhoagland.wordpress.com) and provides material for his province's Web site available at www.thepassionists.org.

He is a member of St. Michael's community in Union City, New Jersey and helps out at St. Mary's Church in Colts Neck, New Jersey.